T0023469

lifeline

lifeline

An Elegy

Stephanie Kain

This book is also available as a Global Certified Accessible™ (GCA) ebook. ECW Press's ebooks are screen reader friendly and are built to meet the needs of those who are unable to read standard print due to blindness, low vision, dyslexia, or a physical disability.

Purchase the print edition and receive the ebook free. For details, go to ecwpress.com/ebook.

Copyright © Stephanie Kain, 2023

Published by ECW Press
665 Gerrard Street East
Toronto, Ontario, Canada M4M 1Y2
416-694-3348 / info@ecwpress.com

All rights reserved. No part of this publication may be reproduced, stored in a retrieval system, or transmitted in any form by any process — electronic, mechanical, photocopying, recording, or otherwise — without the prior written permission of the copyright owners and ECW Press. The scanning, uploading, and distribution of this book via the internet or via any other means without the permission of the publisher is illegal and punishable by law. Please purchase only authorized electronic editions, and do not participate in or encourage electronic piracy of copyrighted materials. Your support of the author's rights is appreciated.

Editor for the Press: Pia Singhal
Copy editor: Shannon Parr
Cover design: David A. Gee

To the best of her abilities, the author has related experiences, places, people, and organizations from her memories of them. In order to protect the privacy of others, she has, in some instances, changed the names of certain people and details of events and places.

LIBRARY AND ARCHIVES CANADA CATALOGUING IN PUBLICATION

Title: Lifeline : an elegy / Stephanie Kain.

Names: Kain, Stephanie, author.

Identifiers: Canadiana (print) 2023023710X | Canadiana (ebook) 20230237134

ISBN 978-1-77041-731-1 (softcover)
ISBN 978-1-77852-211-6 (Kindle)
ISBN 978-1-77852-210-9 (PDF)
ISBN 978-1-77852-209-3 (ePub)

Subjects: LCSH: Kain, Stephanie. | LCSH: Caregivers—Canada—Biography. | LCSH: Depressed persons—Care—Canada. | LCSH: Bipolar disorder. | LCGFT: Autobiographies.

Classification: LCC RC516 .K32 2023 | DDC 616.890092—dc23

This book is funded in part by the Government of Canada. Ce livre est financé en partie par le gouvernement du Canada. We acknowledge the support of the Canada Council for the Arts. Nous remercions le Conseil des arts du Canada de son soutien. We acknowledge the funding support of the Ontario Arts Council (OAC), an agency of the Government of Ontario. We also acknowledge the support of the Government of Ontario through the Ontario Book Publishing Tax Credit, and through Ontario Creates.

ONTARIO ARTS COUNCIL
CONSEIL DES ARTS DE L'ONTARIO
an Ontario government agency
un organisme du gouvernement de l'Ontario

Canada Council for the Arts

Conseil des arts du Canada

Canada

PRINTED AND BOUND IN CANADA

PRINTING: MARQUIS   5 4 3 2 1

This book is made of paper from well-managed FSC® - certified forests, recycled materials, and other controlled sources.

MIX
Paper from responsible sources
FSC® C103567

PCF

BIO GAS

PERMANENT

"We are all searching for someone whose demons play well with ours."

— Heidi R. Kling

Hey, doll,

The rain on Curaçao smells the same as it does at home.

Funny, I thought it would be different. Tinged with palm or something, but it's not. The rainy season extends to February, but the sun has been shining most days, even through heavy clouds. No hurricanes this far south, though.

Usually, I can count on the sun to start to ebb past the numbness of winter and put the spark of motivation back in my body. Press the start button on all the ideas and connections. I love holidays for the simple recharging — the way the ocean, with its incessant rhythms, makes me feel small and helps me bring order to the chaos in my brain.

Eight days in and I'm still waiting for the give-a-fuck to return. I guess my batteries were dead. No ETA on when this reboot might be complete. In the meantime, chasing iguanas, taking pictures. Taking long walks in shallow water.

Maybe it's age or motherhood, or the sheer depth of depression you can reach when you find a way to turn off your anger and realise, slowly, that you've turned off everything else, too. Caring isn't as selective as I once thought. It's engaged or it's not. Kind of a scary idea. Trump's in office. The world is spinning in its own vitriol. And I'm on a beach in the Caribbean with my wife, post-calling-off-the-divorce, writing to you about the sand and the lagoons, trying not to think too far ahead.

In the long hours I've spent not working — and listening to the child's increasing obsession with Disney princesses and happily-ever-afters — I've had second (third, tenth, hundred-fold) doubts about life. Questioning everything, but especially if you can ever really rebuild something you purposely blew up. And if I'm right about happiness being a choice — a collection of choices — something we can work toward, even with all our past mistakes looming in the background of every look and conversation.

I see the fuchsia flowers blooming. The leaves, the trees waxing green. The spotted geckos flitting in and out of holes. Life unfolding day by day. And I try to follow its example. Trust something bigger than my own small decisions.

1

I know things aren't easy for you right now, and I wish I was there to sit with you and tell you I'm proud of you for getting up every single time. For pushing through and getting help, even if it feels like you're losing a fight. I'd like to remind you in person that this isn't the first time the monster in the closet has gotten loose — that you've got combat gear stored away and that you know how to use the stun gun to wrestle it back into its cage. That the best way out is through — straight down the long dark middle. And that I'm always on the other end of the line — morning or night.

This winter will end, and you will still be standing.

Lots of love and sunshine. See you soon. xo

"Take me back to the (day) we met."
— Lord Huron, "The Night We Met"

If we could rewind back to that moment and just. not. meet.
Would you do it?

You could have been fully booked.
I could have chickened out of treatment.

On that day I first
walked into the clinic and your receptionist asked me for my
next of kin,
when my stomach dropped because I wasn't sure if your
small-town practice
ever saw women who answered "my wife" . . .

I could have just walked out.

You could have not made me laugh, and I could have not made you cry, and
we could have never held hands or saved each other.

We could have never created this lifeline we needed to pull you out of those
deep pits you kept finding.

You could be happy right now in your undisturbed life. I could be happy right
now, too.

But my soul would still ache for you, I think.

And your life would still suffocate you.

And your unmined traumas would probably have still hit you like a freight
train, and you might still be where you are right now.

Because it happened before I got there. And it happened after I left.

Someone, not me, could still be sending you care packages on the psych ward
because you aren't allowed visitors and it's COVID anyway.

No guarantees that giving it all up would have saved you all this grief. Or me.

But still . . . if I'd known what a long road it would be. How many trenches we would have to dig,

> and the nights without speaking,
> and the days without knowing . . .

I might just cancel it all.

For once, say no.

I guess it all depends on how this ends.

Empaths Anonymous

Is this your first meeting? Don't worry — everyone's very nice. I just want to give you a little heads-up that if you sit next to me, you might find yourself telling me your story. You might not want to, but I might ask you a simple question that leads to a mild observation and then to an insight and you might start pouring your darkest secrets into my lap and then wondering what the hell just happened.

It's not your fault. I'm part witch. I just thought I'd let you know so you could decide if you really wanted to sit there.

Honestly, I don't know why people tell me their things, but they do all the time, and now I'm going to tell you my things because I think it's only fair. Since you're sitting here now, you're about to start feeling really vulnerable, and that's not your fault, and it's not my fault, but it's a fact, so . . .

Counsellor: Okay, we're going to leap in here, everyone. Steph, do you want to start?

Me: Hi. Yes, sure. My name is Steph. I'm thirty-seven years old and I live on Prince Edward Island. That's in the middle of the ocean next to Canada, for those who aren't familiar with our red shores. I have a wife and a seven-year-old daughter. After getting my PhD in creative writing I decided I didn't want to teach and bought a former goat café, which I turned into a bookstore and coffee shop. I have conflicting core feelings about my career. Sometimes I feel shame about not using my education better, and sometimes I feel relief and gratitude that my life is my own and I don't have to deal with the stress of trying to be a woman on tenure track at a university.

My superpower is active listening. My diagnosis is anxiety/depression, but I have recently tapered off my Cipralex because of the side effects, particularly fatigue and forgetting what sex is. I'm coping at about an eight lately, trending slightly manic, which I feel is a normal, healthy response to this global virus crisis.

I am a writer. Sometimes a counsellor — but in the unregulated, meet-me-for-a-cup-of-tea kind of way.

Counsellor: Thank you. Anyone else?

It's your turn now. Sorry about that. But don't worry. Everyone here is really nice.

Come in. Stay.

I land from Curaçao and come straight to the office we share because two weeks of family time post-calling-off-the-divorce has been the hardest thing and the best thing and the worst thing and you've always been the darkest, most familiar thing, so I put on my professional clothes over my new tan and pick up my laptop and come sit at my desk.

While I was away, you took time out from your own patients and went to the doctor, and she put you back on the meds from the last time, but it's been a few days now and your brain is being flooded with serotonin, which it is apparently rejecting like bad blood. Something about the early menopause and the added decade since the Train Tracks means that the meds are not working the same as before, and when I finally get back, you're lying down on the treatment tables between patients and I'm watching you from the doorway, trying to decide if I should call someone. But who would I call now?

I wasn't around for your first breakdown, but you've told me about the long days spent on the floor with crippling back pain, the slow climb out of the fog, the medication that made you softer but slower, and the way you painted yourself back to health. The painting of the blue heron that hangs in my office is a talisman of your improvement. I look at it carefully, trying to imagine you sitting still long enough to create something so intricate. I can't.

But now, you come to my door, as if you need to ask to come in. As if you've ever needed to ask. Still, I look up from my work and push my glasses to the top of my head, and I don't say, *well get in here for shit's sake* because something in your face warns me that you are not the same person I left and that it's taking everything you have not to lie down on the floor in the middle of the room, so instead I tell you gently to sit down. Rest.

I give you my writing shawl and you drape it over your shoulders and push the recliner all the way back, and I go back to work, half-watching you as I type replies to two weeks' worth of requests for extensions.

This is the first time I watch you sleeping and for a moment you seem okay — though I probably shouldn't say okay, because the person I left would have been up a ladder at noon on a weekday, not ever sitting, eyes closed, in the corner of my office, hiding from her charting and the ringing of the phone. So you're clearly not okay, even if you look . . . sleepy?

I've given up on email and am googling side effects of the Celexa you're taking when you suddenly sit up, the footrest of the chair crashing into the frame. You shake your head, your loose curls bouncing despite all the hairspray, and you breathe out, a short hollow breath.

"I'm freaking out."

I lean back in my chair. "Okay."

"It's not good."

"Okay." Pause. Think. What should we do? "Do you want to go to the hospital?"

You look at me, weighing the possibility. "I don't know. What would they do?"

I feel like a lightning pole, discharging the electricity in the room before it can reach you.

"I don't know. Change your meds, maybe?"

I close my laptop and swivel my chair toward you — note the fear in your face and the way you're sitting like you've been shocked by the recliner.

"Do you want to go for a walk?"

"I don't have time, do I?"

And I lean forward with my elbows on my knees, just watching you. The waves of not-good ripple outward like vibrating rings, and I can see you cracking along the seams. You sit, trying to breathe, but your body is shaking and I feel it in my own body — the fear like a tap on full blast that we just need to turn off — so I stand up and walk over to you, hold out my hands.

You look up, your eyes pleading with me not to make you move, but you take my hands and I pull you to your feet.

I don't know what makes me think it's okay or what you need or what you want but I put my arms around you and hold you — not too tight, but tight enough — and you don't pull away or ask me *what the fuck* but put your face into my shoulder because, with my heels on, we're the same height.

And I rub your back and say over and over in a low voice, "It's going to be okay." And you hold me like you're dying. And when it's time to let go, you don't.

That was the start.

Or Maybe It Wasn't

Maybe the start was when I was pregnant and the only person I saw for nine months besides my wife and my OB was you because you could put my body back together when the baby was stretching it apart at the ligaments and I was too sick to get off the couch even though I was working full time as an online professor and you used to grin at me coming in the door and my heart used to flip over and . . .

(Even when you said something about a beached whale in my ninth month and made me cry.)

Or maybe it was when my daughter was one and you were the only one who could see I was being bludgeoned with Postpartum because everyone talked about the Depression kind and not the Anxiety kind, but you could see it from 100 paces and you said, "Be careful, sweetie. Call me." And when it didn't get better, you cleared out the back office at the clinic and helped me move my stuff in, pretending not to peek in on me while I marked midterms. And your patients waved at me, hesitantly, as they passed by my door because they weren't quite sure what a writer might be doing there or why you looked at me like that.

But probably it was that day when I was looking at the letter from the cryogenic lab where our extra sperm was stored and crying because I couldn't bring myself to check the box to tell them to flush it but I also knew deep in my soul that I couldn't survive another pregnancy, and you pulled my wife into a treatment room and told her that having another baby would wreck me. That the toll it would take on my body and mind wasn't worth it and that she needed to tell me it was okay to be done. And something changed — reversed. You stepped into the role of my protector, full combat gear, and I let you. I wanted you to. Why? I don't know. I never knew I needed protecting. Not from her, not from the world. But that's what happened. And I never wanted to change it back.

That was the start.

Zoom Therapy, Day One

Me: How are you?

Counsellor: Doing very well today, thanks.

Me: If you're doing very well during a pandemic, you're either a psychopath or a liar. I'm not sure which one I prefer in a therapist.

Counsellor: (laughs) Okay, well, I'm doing as well as can be expected then.

Me: Thank you for your honesty. I appreciate that.

Counsellor: When did you first realise that you had a superpower?

Me: When I was a child.

Counsellor: So young?

Me: Yeah. Very young. Adults would talk to me about all their problems. Sometimes they would cry.

Counsellor: Did that scare you?

Me: Not really.

The head of pottery at camp with the abusive ex-husband

> *My best friend's mom who had MS and worried about when she couldn't turn the pages of a book anymore*

>> *My teacher who killed herself*

Counsellor: Tell me about that.

Me: Miss Cross?

Counsellor: Was that her name?

Me: She was very young. It was her first year teaching. At the time, I thought it was our fault because we were really awful students. But now, looking back, I can see the context. What might've led to her decision.

Counsellor: Were you awful?

Me: I wasn't the worst, but I didn't help.

She left school in the middle of the day and didn't come back for our Latin class. Instead, we made puppets from felt with the vice principal while everyone ran around trying to find out where the hell she'd gone.

Counsellor: How did it happen?

Me: She stopped taking her insulin. She left town first, though, which is why it took so long to find her.

One day, little Jacqueline came running into the room to say she'd been found, and Mrs. Jasper had to sit down she was so relieved. She just kept saying Thank God.

And then the principal came in to say it was a false report. She was still missing.

Counsellor: She died by diabetic coma?

Me: Yes. She even put on a snowsuit first because she knew she would be cold. It took them weeks to find her.

Counsellor: That takes some planning.

Me: Yes.

Our parents wouldn't let us watch the news because the media kept talking about how decomposed she was when she was found.

Counsellor: And what context do you see now?

Me: Well, I mean, I can see how the compounding problems just kept piling up: her fiancé had broken up with her, her diabetes was quite severe, her dream of being a teacher was not going well. I can see why she did it, but I wish I'd been able to help. I talked to her once after class. She was so grateful for the conversation. And then the next day I acted like I didn't even know her. I was embarrassed.

Counsellor: And now?

Me: I guess now it's an ACE.

Counsellor: What are your other ACEs?

Me: This is a fifty-minute session, right?

Counsellor: Listen, I'm not judging. It's not like you chose them for yourself.

Me: Yes. Maybe.

Counsellor: Well, they can become tools but first they must be named. What was it? Abuse? Trauma?

Me: Honestly, I don't know how to answer that.

Counsellor: Just think back on the shitty things and tell them to me.

Me: Fine. There was a lot of screaming in my house. A lot of hitting. A lot of threats of violence and a lot of isolation. And I just counted down the days until I could run away.

Counsellor: How did you cope?

Me: I just lived there.

Counsellor: But people in maladaptive situations maladapt. So, what did you do to self-destruct?

Me: I cut myself.

Counsellor: Why?

Me: Because it stopped my brain from counting.

Counsellor: Like OCD counting?

Me: Like whatever twelve-year-olds with anxiety do, I guess.

Counsellor: Tell me about it.

Me: I don't want to.

Counsellor: Do it anyway. You make everyone else tell you their stories. It's your turn.

Me: I'd rather tell their stories. The light is too bright on mine. I'd rather give away the page space.

Counsellor: Don't you think that's part of the problem? Pick up the pen then.

Me: Fine.

I am addicted to chaos.

> I keep the worst-case scenario safely secreted at the very centre of my mind. Intrusive thoughts contained in a bomb-proof shelter. Fear the worst and then it can't happen.

I cannot bear it when people are glib with their happiness. I prefer it when they hedge it, cautiously. Even in books, I hate happy protagonists. I think they deserve the anvils of misfortune that come crashing down.

Happiness leads to disappointment. Don't be disappointed. Don't be happy.

Counsellor: What else?

Me: Aren't we done yet for fuck's sake?

Counsellor: I don't know. Are we? Isn't it all heavy? Just throw it all at the wall.

Me: Fine. Okay. Here you go: Yes, OCD-type counting. I used to count my steps. I used to be afraid of the knives in the kitchen drawer downstairs because I was afraid I'd use them to hurt myself. I used to be afraid of the gun my father kept in the attic because I was afraid I'd sneak up there in the middle of the night and use it to kill myself. Most of all, I was afraid of bulimia. Because I was afraid of vomiting.

Counsellor: Tell me about the knives.

Me: I never used them. I waited for the razors.

Counsellor: Oh, so no Capital-T trauma then?

Me: Fuck off.

Counsellor: Right.

Me: I just gave in and started cutting my wrists. Because it didn't hurt as much as obsessing about it. Okay? Are you happy now?

Counsellor: Finally. Jesus. I've never met someone so hard to help.

Me: Have you looked in the mirror lately?

Show Me Your ACEs

Adverse Childhood Experiences (ACEs):
traumatic events which occur in childhood
and which can negatively impact one's
well-being and mental health in adulthood.

Shame drags across
my skin, sharp like the pointed
barbs she spits.
Don't fight back, just
swallow it.
Don't try to
deflect the never-ending
sneers,
the things that make her hate you.

Lazy
      Fat
            Hysterical
      Dramatic
Queer

Drag a little more,
the too-dull razor that she
laughed about.
Why would anyone use a safety razor on their wrists?
Jeering, spitting with rage and
laughter, both
as she read my diary aloud
to the table: her new husband,
his teenage children, looking at their plates,
cheeks red.

Shame starts early.
In some cases, buried deep under
a pile of ACEs.

Only therapy can properly mine the
source but
I have a pretty good idea where
my shame began.

Shh. Be quiet for God's sake.
Stop licking your lips like that, it's disgusting.
You're too much.
Stop talking. Stop laughing.
WILL YOU STOP MAKING SO MUCH FUCKING NOISE?!

Looking sideways at my
stomach,
my thighs,
shouting if cookies went
missing from
the cupboard,
dragging me downstairs, out of bed,
to answer for the missing Quality Streets.

Half a glass of juice a day!
No ice cream after school!

Being fat perhaps the most egregious sin of all
next to Pride?

When I fit a size 6 that summer after camp, canoeing and kayaking in the
heat, no matter that they were the ugliest jeans in the store, gleefully holding
them up, like I'd finally brought home a prize.

Straight-As not counted.
Because once, long ago, there had been a C.
When?
I don't know.
It all blends together: years of late nights and studying
and crying over tests and
crying over grades and
saying no to parties and no to dances and no to everything
partly because I didn't like the boys
but also because I liked my math teacher better
and she liked me. But not that way . . .

Or maybe a bit that way, on my side, but I was sixteen and
she was twenty-five and
new and . . . I don't know now.

But wow did she ever hit the roof and rain down on that
whole school, ripping it all apart like
my first manuscripts. Like my first journals.
Packaging them up and sending them to the
headmistress.

See? Look what you've done to my daughter.

Them? Really?

The looks.
Horror and pity and fear and . . .
My whole world slowly
fading into the background
until I was left on the sidewalk outside.

Have you ever had a safe space?
Yes. Once. School. Before the hurricane arrived.

Graduation denied.
All the music silenced.
Finishing my OACs at that run-down
public high school, putting its
STAMP on the rest of my life
like that boy who left his ring of teeth on the inside of my thigh.

What a waste.
Fucking waste of
four years of work.

And my poor teacher who . . .

Her life could have been ruined.

Just because she . . .
What?
Nothing.

Nothing.

Later, after the pregnancy weight
came off and I just kept losing it —

not because I was trying or
because I wanted to but
because of the stress
and the insomnia
and the baby with all her needs
and the never-ever-fucking-sleeping,
she flashed me a warm smile,
praising a dog after obedience class,
finally getting the jumps right.

She didn't ask about the constant running or
the almost-affair or the
meds or the crying.

She gave me her expensive leather coats from Italy as a prize.

Take my love. Swallow it. Be happy.
Swallow the way you looked at him:
That hate _like a brick coming at him_, he said,
the way he flung you on the
floor and beat you
and chased you down the hall and
the way he set after you at the park
looking like the pit bull he once
saved you from, frothing and angry,
cuffed you in the cheek over and over
in the face
and the way he doesn't
remember now, in his old age
seventeen years estrangement
and he's in your inbox,
in your kitchen,
telling you no, no, that didn't happen.

No, you don't remember.

What? No, you don't have an Aunt Mary.
You can't because I would remember.

Looking at him like he's an alien,
because he is, really,
from another time.
Out of sync with this one.
A time traveller photo-bombing your present.

But he brings with him a bouquet of ACEs and asks to be let in.

Long winter mornings
at the track,
breathing in the freezing air
and skating away from the looks
your mother gave you.

You have to be the best.
You have to beat them.

We were raised by wolves
you used to say — a little shrug
and quirk of the mouth like
it didn't matter,
ever loyal to the yoke.

You meant you
raised yourselves
but that discounts the razor
teeth and sharp snarls,
the way mothers
carry their cubs
by the scruff of the neck.

Training, training for those five
interlocking rings only to fall grabbing them.

And then . . .

What happened?
Why did you come home?

Your dad says you burned your lungs
out in a race on the prairies, that you got mono,
but you say,

I just . . . I had no support.

The same thing that would follow you
from relationship to relationship all
your life until, finally, you couldn't take
the loneliness because . . .

There was just no affection.

Competition is not love.

At college, late, you perfected the
art of the exam and
valedictorian grades and you were
the life of the party and
the girl who laughed and
the girl who danced and
the girl who fucked.

Have a margarita. It's okay.
Everything's okay.

Your boyfriend from college told you
if he ever had an accident, if ever
he was impaired,
tell them to pull the plug.

And then had an aneurysm
days later.
Catastrophic, but not fatal.
And his parents came and took him
away.
Kept him plugged in.
Cut you off without a word.

Closure denied.

So you didn't marry him.
Or the man who left you for
Europe.

Or the man after that who . . . never mind,
we don't have to talk about that.

It's fucked. I'm fucked.

No, you're not, doll. But he was.

You just didn't realise.

Shh, it's okay. There's nothing wrong with you.
That wasn't your fault, what he did.
You didn't deserve that.

You've run out of time. You've
finished graduate school and
Established Yourself
and you're a doctor now; you've done
all the avoiding you can do.
You're still from a small
Ontario town, you know.
People will talk if you . . .

It's time. C'mon.

Your mother is suicidal so your father
asks you to come home.

I need you. I don't know what to do with her.
Give her something to do, please . . .

Plan a wedding?

A white lace veil,
hair high like you'd stepped right out
of Texas,
makeup and nail polish that you'd
never wear again

And the pressure of him, between
your legs and in your head,
faster, better, harder, higher

Finally drives you to stop trying to
outrun the train and instead just
lie down on the tracks.

But I'm not that way.

I know. I know you're
not that way.
Do you understand what you're saying?

Pushing the lid of that tea canister
in and out and in and out while the
words come halt.ing.ly, pain.ful.ly.

The expectation.

I feel so bad for him, but I just can't.

If You're Searching for Causes . . .

We think it was the Pill.
The one you took for contraception and
later endometriosis and
later habit because
popping pills is just so
rote, why change?

But we don't know.

We say that because it all happened at once,
and it's hard to say
which was the chicken,
which was the egg, and
what made the giant
scrambled mess.

The loneliness and the hormones and the anxiety
and the separation and the uncertainty and the whispering
all collided and
that monster came knocking.

Why?

Because it had been ten years since it had
paid a visit?

Because it smelled an opening: a crack
in the armour. The tender spot
I'd left unguarded
at your back when I left?

Because it had been silently swimming in the
fissures of your brain for years?

Because it knew that this time,
you were older,
you couldn't run as fast,
you couldn't distract yourself as well,
you couldn't wrestle it back to the netherworld?

I don't know.

We fought it with SSRIs
and walks and SNRIs and puzzles and
NDRIs and talking and
finally sleeping pills to give you some
goddamn rest.

But you were shaky and pale and
exhausted beyond exhausted.

Constantly running from a stalker
who was calling from inside the house.

I stopped working downstairs in my office.
Instead I just came straight up to the flat every
morning to check you'd made it through the night.

Close the door. Hold you until you could breathe again.

No, nobody's watching. You're okay.

To Do:

- *Shower*
- *Clothes*
- *Hair*
- *Makeup*
- *Shoes*

Deep breaths. Eat this. You can do it.

                                You're my lifeline right now, Steph.

I know. I'm here.

Most days, you could do it.

Even if, before or after, we were walking up to the medical clinic to add or subtract a pill or a cream or a sedative. Even if you stopped being able to remember what you were on and what you'd gone off and I'd started to keep a notebook in the living room with your medication summaries and a calendar of appointments and you started to be scared about the side effects or even if you were living in reality at all.

- ~~*Celexa*~~
- ~~*SEROQUEL*~~
- *Remeron (keep for now)*
- ~~*Effexor*~~
- ~~*Wellbutrin*~~
- *Lorazepam (doc says no more refills)*
- *Abilify* ✓

And we started to wonder just when we should pull the plug on your workday and what the fuck would happen to you if we did . . .

And then that counsellor said, hey, maybe it wasn't depression. Maybe it was worse! Suicidal OCD. That would make sense!

And you came out of the appointment, shoved the information packet at me, and walked home.

And I read it and I saw it and I said, maybe. *It might make sense? Does it make sense to you?*

And that's when you lost it.

Shirley MacLaine Is a Verb

How do you help someone get psychiatric care in Canada? How do you not stand and watch them slip through the cracks of universal healthcare, but instead, in the middle of their blind freefall, shove them hard enough to land miraculously on the X of proper treatment?

Maybe it depends on whether or not you've seen *Terms of Endearment* and can replicate Shirley MacLaine's performance — if you can ball your hands into fists and swallow hard and reject everything you've ever been taught about being a woman in the world and sitting quietly and waiting your turn; if you can ignore the other patients in the waiting room, staring at you slack-jawed because you Shirley MacLaine-ing is the most fascinating/horrifying thing that's happened to them all day. (And it's been a long day watching the slow rotation of other patients in and out of the bullring. Never them.)

Maybe this is only one way. Maybe this is the only way.

Because if you *can't*, then when you bring somebody into the ER after a suicide attempt, you will be redirected to Chairs, where you will wait for eight hours, one of the Watchers. Not seen. Not heard. Then, in the pre-dawn hours, after a safety contract has been half-heartedly waved around, and everyone is on the verge of collapse from the dehydrated, sanitized air and having sat upright on uncomfortable, hard-backed chairs through the night, you will have to take her back home to cope with her intrusive suicidal thoughts without help and without sleep.

Days will pass and she'll be there again. Because — *why wouldn't she be there again if the job didn't get done the first time?*

So this time, if you *can* — if you can put on your warrior boots and kick down the door of Expected Behaviour in a Hospital; if you've spent days and weeks of your life in pediatric ICUs and geriatric ICUs and you know nurses by floor and by name and by blood type, and you've learned the mechanics and hierarchy of not just one hospital but every hospital, and you also grew up with a mother who hated any sign of illness or histrionics that even smelled like a mental health condition (but at least taught you the value of a good old-fashioned public tantrum), then yes, you will march your suicidal girlfriend up to the glass window and bang on it, and when the triage nurse asks you to take a seat, you — the normally mild-mannered, empathic, bespectacled English professor — will find yourself shouting, No. We will NOT sit down. *She was already SENT to sit down when her father brought her on Monday, and then you people sent her HOME and she almost DIED today.*

And the nurse, who you can tell is normally very calm and probably even somewhat jaded and eye-rolling under regular circumstances will say, *You don't have to get upset,* and you will roar back, *I'm not upset. I'm terrified. She just tried to have herself run over by a Mack truck. I can't keep her safe anymore. You have to help her now.*

And the nurse will nod and buzz you into the bullring and speak gently to you both and when she says, *It sounds like you've been having a very rough time,* you'll wonder how many people just like your girlfriend she sees every day, and if they bother putting the Dr. in front of their names on their charts when they become patients, or if even that's wiped away from them because they've accidentally swallowed this poison that begins to turn their thoughts black.

And the nurse, who regards you a little less warily now that you've admitted that you're scared and not homicidal, and has seen the tears collecting under the lenses of the sunglasses you're wearing indoors because the halogens are so fucking bright, will look you more or less in the eye now. Even when she's telling you, gently but firmly, *I really need her to answer for herself.* You don't argue to tell that nurse that when she answers for herself she might be lying, like this morning when she saw patients for five hours, then told you she was going for a haircut, but instead drove out to the highway.

In the small side room, you'll wait for a psych nurse to come down. And, like dropping your Method acting on the floor after the director calls *cut,* you will emerge bleary-eyed from your Shirley MacLaine impersonation and try to remember what happened.

What the fuck has just happened?

You remember reading the note and flying out the door just as she was pulling back into the driveway, tires skidding on the gravel as she abandoned her car sideways at the top of the hill and staggered out. Grabbing her by her hands and looping her arms around your neck.

You told me you were going for a haircut. You said . . .

I know. I know. I'm sorry. I just couldn't do it anymore.

Rocking, rocking, on the bed until she started crying. *I'm sorry. I'm sorry.*

And then what? Then what happened?

I looked at their faces driving by. The truck drivers. I imagined . . . I couldn't do it to them.

Holding her with one arm, hands shaking so hard you could barely dial, trying to call her father. He only worked up the fucking street, for fuck's sake. Again, and again, hearing it go to voicemail, and then finally just putting her in your own car and swerving out onto the highway toward the ER.

Close your eyes.

She does.

You don't want her to see the trucks driving by. You don't want to see them either, but you have to keep the car on the road and your heart is racing so fast you feel sick and jumpy from the adrenaline that you know will precipitate one hell of a fucking headache as soon as you land.

Land.

At the hospital.

WHICH WAY TO THE HOSPITAL?

Driving, one-handed, your other hand holding hers, which feels like a limp, dead fish; you squeeze and feel nothing. Her head lolls against the back of the seat rest. Did she take something too? When? Did you watch her take something? Why can't you remember?

(Years later, you still will not be able to remember even though you will remember every. single. other. detail. of. that. day. Even when you can't stand to remember anymore.)

The rest of it is a blur. The parking lot, the pay ticket, the walk toward the doors. You've checked your phone four times. Where is her dad? Why isn't he picking up? Why didn't they do something when she was here two days ago?

WHERE THE FUCK IS HER DAD? Your wife yells in shouty texts. GIVE ME HIS NUMBER AND I'LL CALL HIM MYSELF.

You need to turn the phone off, but you can't turn the phone off because her dad might call back even though the buzzing, buzzing, buzzing is sending your heart rate through the roof, and you are about to burst into tears.

THIS ISN'T YOUR JOB. YOU HAVE A DAUGHTER TO LOOK AFTER. YOU HAVE YOUR OWN LIFE.

And your face flushes, heat creeping everywhere over your body, your throat closing up again because yes, you have a daughter at home who you're supposed to take swimming today and a wife who loves you as much as she hates you, or almost. Even if, maybe, you U-hauled a little bit. Even if, maybe, you were too young. Even if, maybe, you should have stayed separated after all instead of trying to reconcile the relationship when this — all this — is sitting in the middle of it like a stone fucking elephant.

But the noise and texts and the waiting and the stress and the trying to get in touch with her *fucking father* rises like a cacophony of bird calls and you finally understand the cuckoo's nest. You see how people break. You see how it happened to her: the warrior's back finally slipping a disc and crumbling under the weight of all the things — the house and the practice and the soon-to-be-ex-husband and the toxic leak under the building and the patients, and that small town with their rumours and their gossip, and you . . .

Is it you? Are you the reason? The final straw that pushed her over that knife edge she was already walking?

She is your best friend, your warrior queen, your soft-butch protector and everything but . . . *everything but that*. But those small-town people just see the *everything* and ignore the *but* — then raise eyebrows, whisper, point, speculate about exactly what you are to each other. Population 2,000; churches on every corner and the agricultural fair the highlight of the year . . . how? HOW has she reconciled you with the old/new boyfriend she sees every other weekend. The one whose apartment she's so excited to decorate.

She hasn't. She can't. And she can't not. So here you are.

The years have played out and you hardly recognise her.

You remember her in her three-inch platform heels and tight blue jeans, moving around her exam room, half-smile playing on her lips. You remember her mother dying and her father getting remarried. The way she stopped short when you asked how she was doing, and she didn't know what to say. Nobody ever asked her that. So she just told you the truth, the whole truth, then looked at you in amazement, like you'd done some sort of witchcraft. And you hugged her — that old version of her, a bit surprised when she relaxed into your arms like a rag doll that needed a squeeze. She didn't know how to put her regular armour on again after that, so she didn't bother.

Your walks in the woods, mosquitoes buzzing around your heads so you had to run, flapping your arms around your ears to escape the bugs, and she was laughing, laughing right behind you as you emerged from the treeline because she had no idea you could run like that. No idea that while she was playing soccer and running marathons and doing Mud events that she wasn't the only one who could sprint when it counted.

(And so, in the months after this, when you will walk with her around the block every day, after she moves into her stepmother's house and you go over each morning to help, when she says, because her mind is still a mess of worst-case scenarios, dominated by swirling poisonous thoughts: *If I took off running toward the road, what would you do?* You won't remind her you can damn well outrun her if you need to. You'll just say, *I'd take off my fucking shoe and throw it at your head.* And she'll laugh.)

The phone buzzes and buzzes and you think, really, you're going to have to turn it off even if you haven't gotten in touch with him because your friends are texting you, and her office assistants are texting you, and your wife is TEXTING YOU, and you're two seconds away from screaming but instead you try his number one more time and finally, *finally*, his secretary answers. And you tell her to *get him to the ER now*. And you hang up and *finally* turn off your phone and get back on the gurney next to her because that fucking chair is bolted to the floor, and you can't get it close enough to hold her hand. So you sit at one end, back to the wall, and put the pillow in your lap for her to rest her head on, and run your fingers through her hair and down her back and tell her to breathe, and feel her melting into you, and know that something's gotta give. Something's gotta fucking give because this is all too . . .

Breathe, doll.

Hand gliding up, down, up, down, stopping in the middle to dig your thumbs into that spot between her shoulder blades that makes her moan softly because it's a constant ache with no relief except when you touch her. And that's okay because you're just friends.

You're amazing, you know that?

Just breathe.

The door opens and he finally hurries in, jacket undone, deep lines etched into his forehead, the bridge of his nose. He's not out of breath; he moves like a panther, like she does, and it's hard for you to believe he's in his seventies, this distinguished guy who looks so much like her. Who's given her so much of himself, including his own demons and his own failings. But he just cups her face in his hands, and she bursts into tears, which is such a rarity. Such an odd thing for her. You're so glad to see it. You think, for a moment, there might be hope. And she doesn't get up. Doesn't push away. Just lets her dad see her lying with her head on your lap. Lets him see. Dares him to, almost.

What did you do?

But she just cries, and he holds her face for a while and kisses her forehead and then sits down on the bolted chair and waits. Waits.

When the psych resident comes down, you both sit up and lean back against the wall. You lace your fingers with hers, arms pressed between your bodies, and see the doctor glance down, then back up. Knowing she assumes, and the nurses assume, and letting them assume because it's mostly fucking true anyway. And thinking that finally, if someone sees, someone knows, someone will be able to bring it up with her because nobody else can, including you.

And you want to leave, but you can't because he loves her but he can't Shirley MacLaine. And that's why you're here.

Soulmates

I remember the day we stopped the car. Your eyes were on the road, taking the hairpin turn like it was a ride at an amusement park. Back when you used to drive. Back before you left your husband. When he was out of town and we were out every day, walking and shopping and lunching and laughing. Omg, we laughed. A giddy, light, slightly unhinged laughter because we had untethered the balloon we were standing in and dared it to take us as high as it could, and it did. We were flying. Freefalling and still laughing as we crashed back down.

When you looked at me and said, "He's home tomorrow. We have to stop."

And everything my wife had said to me and everything I'd denied because *for the love of fuck we are not sleeping together* suddenly overwhelmed me and I put my head against the window and asked you, without looking at you, how I was supposed to live in this space where my feelings and your feelings and their feelings just made everything so twisted up and tainted when all we wanted was this space for ourselves in our own box that didn't have a label because there was no word for us, but everybody just kept pointing and glaring and it was getting dangerous, not just for me but for our spouses and my kid and your small-town practice that would have crucified you if they'd been listening in but you said, so simply:

"There is a word for us. We're soulmates."

And my heart stopped a little and the breath rushed out of me in this cold flood of relief because all this time I was trying to figure it out, you knew? You knew and you were right. You'd named it, somehow, when I couldn't.

Of course that explained the way you and I were rooted to the same core so hard I could feel your heart beating.

But I was still surprised you said it.

The town was gossiping, and your husband was hearing it, but he still stood up when I came into the room and nodded at me cordially. Always the Southern gentleman. If it was true, he would have let you go gracefully — taken your hand and put it into mine with a bow and a smile of concession because obviously it had nothing to do with him . . . but you were also seeing another man — did he know that part?

I had a box seat to your marriage and watched the silences grow longer and louder even as you kept smiling, smiling, smiling in all the pictures, until one day, you came back from your twenty-year anniversary trip and didn't bother to unpack your suitcase because you'd known before you left that when you got back you were leaving him, and I helped you pack your things and we loaded them into my trunk — all your goddamned back-breaking shoes you never wore again.

And this time when you were untethered you didn't fly. You ran toward the cliff edge and jumped, expecting your wings to deploy, but they didn't.

They were atrophied, I guess. Stuck. Mechanism failed and you

just

kept

falling.

And years later, drugs on and drugs off, I know I should have said something to you in that moment. That you opened the door, and I froze, too afraid of what lay beyond.

Shut up for fuck's sake.

Don't talk back to me.

A lifetime of words stick in my throat and

I

can't

speak.

So I just breathe out and you glance at me, silent, and keep driving until we're home.

We weren't sleeping together but that didn't matter. Maybe we should have just given in and taken each other's clothes off.

Our bare skin colliding might have been less of a betrayal to everyone.
Honest, at least.

Because what good is a body in a marriage
without a soul?

You're sad and you can't hide it from me and that scares you. In the quiet hours before your afternoon patients start arriving, we sit in my office, and I make us some tea and wait. But you can't say the words yet, even if you need someone to feel them with you. The weight of your marriage is too great and it's starting to push your feet down into the ground that's softer than it seemed before. You can feel the movement of the earth and don't know how far in you're going to sink. The loose ends of life are beginning to wind themselves together into a knot you suspect you won't be able to unravel. You're losing yourself. You're losing your progress.

"I don't want to break again," you say quietly.

And I squeeze your hand.

Build Me an Attic

Do you remember when I rediscovered the abandoned third floor of your Victorian office building? Two floors above the main level where you worked in your crashing practice and I shut the door of my corner office against the smell of Biofreeze and the thrum of the TENS machine, hidden through another door at the back of your soon-to-be-flat, and up another long, creaky staircase . . . it had been there all along, over our heads while we worked, day in and day out, but you'd just never grabbed my hand to climb the stairs.

The peeling paint and dead bugs made it look like something directly out of Ontario Abandoned Places. I used to browse pictures in my spare time because I was fascinated with haunted old asylums.

That was long before I began to associate you with places like that.

When you were just you and I was just me and our days were punctuated with jokes and laughter and adventure instead of trips to the ER and supervised walks to the pharmacy. When we still went to lunch at chic places and you still drove with one hand on the wheel, smiling at me while we talked.

Before our relationship became entirely wrapped up in your illness.

There was a breaking-and-entering raccoon that summer, and you were afraid to look into the cage to see if he had been caught, but you were such an animal lover, even for those pests, that you couldn't stand leaving it alone in the baking sun on the flat tarmac roof. Trap-and-release, the guy had promised you, so we climbed those long, steep stairs to check the trap and — fuck, yes, if that animal wasn't already half faint with heat stroke.

And while we were waiting for the guy to come for the release-after-catch, I looked around in wonder at the grime-covered windows, the ancient threadbare carpet. The blue/green Formica kitchenette that was straight out of the '40s, and that mermaid with obscenely red hair painted on the wall of the microscopic bathroom.

"That's not one of mine," you said with your classic lip twitch.

"Really?" I shot you a grin.

"Former tenant."

"Someone lived up here? Recently?"

"A few years now, but yeah."

"This place is amazing."

You looked at me like I was cruising for a psychotic break.

But I could see it already . . .

I sent you a picture from Pinterest of a renovated attic space: soft mauve walls and white furniture, an orchid, a bohemian rug. Your place was better. It could be an oasis.

You're more than a wife and a doctor, and you deserve your own space to breathe.

You didn't answer me, but outside my doorway, at your own desk, you sat quietly, staring at your screen. Then you started your own board, and we began to pin.

Later, you and your then-husband threw the stove off the third-storey roof down to the gravel driveway below, and it hit with an almighty bang that would have scared every animal for a ten-mile radius, and, on its way down, the corner clipped you in the side, knocking you off balance. You almost fell.

What if you'd just fallen?

What if, instead of slowly sliding down the long, slippery hill to the bottom over months and years, what if you'd just taken one flying leap off that third-storey roof and been done?

We start off with cleaning. Ripping up the carpet, vacuuming up the thousands of chevron beetles and house flies that have chosen this hill to die on. We sweep and wash the walls. I crawl into the little alcoves and clean the windows so the sunlight comes back in. You rip out the kitchenette and throw it overboard.

It's bare. Empty. A blank slate.

"I'm going to leave him," you say.

I look at you, note the quiet way you say it. Just an idea you think you're testing out for the first time in open air. But you've made your decision.

"I know."

You stop. "How? I didn't even know."

I left my wife three months ago. She thinks I'm sleeping with you. You're leaving your husband now. Will he think the same thing?

You're in a t-shirt and old pants, painter's cap, and bare face. You don't look a thing like I'm used to, but I like you better this way.

You look around the space, stripped bare and waiting for something big to happen to it. "Are you going to live up here?"

"It's too small. I'll live on the second floor. You can work up here."

At IKEA, we park in the underground and walk into the largest store in Canada like it's an exciting adventure except that you are barely keeping up, and I have to lead you by the fastest route to the kitchen section.

You're replaying the scene in your mind, over and over: him begging you not to leave, you letting go of his hand. You've left your home now, and that's harder than you thought. Even though you no longer have to lie beside him every night, not breathing, not moving. Even though you're absolved of the expectation, the pretense, the secrets. Even still . . . you miss your life. The woods. The ridge. The décor you've collected from all your travels. The view at night.

You wish he'd been the one to leave but you know he never would have.

It's taken a toll — losing your house. Learning you'll have to pay him alimony because . . . ? Because. We're not sure.

You're sleeping on a mattress in a friend's basement because the second floor isn't ready, and the dogs can't make it up here to the almost-finished loft that you're still trying to finish because you want something happy. A fireplace straight out of a Pinterest picture.

So we go up to the kitchen section. You stare blankly at all the panels, and I point to the drawings, the measurements.

Your eyes are unfocused, something not computing.

It's too much — too much change, too many expectations, too much freefalling. And this task, this thing that's supposed to keep you chained to the earth, is splintering you.

"I'm sorry. It just doesn't make sense to me."

"It's okay. That's why I'm here."

I order the right number of panels in each size, and you pick the shiny knobs, and then we go for tea and cake at the food court because your brain is shorting out and you still need to drive us home.

You pick a soft grey for the walls and dark hardwood floors. Yellow accents and a giant nest chair like the one I ~~have~~ had at home . . . a grey couch and fancy sconces, soft rugs, and the throw blanket I give you for a housewarming.

It's beautiful. It's perfect.

But by the time it's done, you've not only left your husband, you've also set your whole life on fire.

Not to mention mine.

Swallow It

"Brother, let me be your fortress
When the night wheels are driving on
Be the one to light the way
Bring you home."
– Needtobreathe, "Brother"

I: Medication

The door closes behind the nurse, and I sit on the small metal chair covered in a burgundy tweed. This chair moves freely — it is not bolted to the floor. I move it half an inch toward the wall, just to enjoy moving it. To double-check that my reality hasn't changed that much. That, normally, chairs still move, and doors still open without a buzzer. Then I wait, trying to keep my hands still.

The smell of hand sanitizer and cotton swabs is now as familiar to me as the smells of my own kitchen.

I don't like hospitals. I don't like doctors' offices. And yet, I've lost track of the number of waiting rooms I've been in over the past few weeks. Maybe it's been months.

The door opens and Deena slams in, bringing with her a scent cloud of Middle Eastern cooking. Her hair is a formidable black, like octopus ink. When she speaks, garlic rolls off her tongue along with her thick Iraqi accent. Although she wears black tights and old-lady Oxfords with her white coat, she is young and quick to smile. Her lipstick is a slash of pink on her face, which is otherwise un-made-up.

We've seen each other frequently enough this year that I can tell she's had a haircut. I wonder if she's married. Where she lives. How many times today the secretary has reminded her that *here*, she's just a doctor's assistant. Because she's chosen not to be *there* anymore, and this is the price she tacitly agreed to pay. Somehow, I'm sure she hadn't factored these deliberate daily slights into that decision. I wonder if she ever regrets it.

Deena: How is the vertigo?

She always sits and looks at me so frankly that I am afraid I have something on my face. But I've discovered over the past year that she has a wicked sense of humour and I like to hear her laugh.

Me: Well, since I tried cutting out salt and attending a prayer meeting, it has almost completely gone away.

She stares at me, and I stare back deadpan before we both laugh.

Deena: No! She didn't actually suggest that! She can't have said it out loud.

She runs a hand through her wiry black hair and I notice that it *does* move when she touches it. She pulls a face and shakes her head as if she wants to scream.

Deena: She's going to give me a breakdown. I'm not joking. She has to stop giving advice to people. She just works at the front desk. What if she kills somebody? Who's going to get the blame?

Me: He should fire her.

Deena: He can't fire his wife.

Me: She is literally terrible. She won't even open the window to patients to take their information and then she makes you announce your complaints to the entire clinic. I don't know how you work with her.

She closes her eyes and takes a breath, then refocuses her attention on me.

Deena: Well, if cutting salt and attending a prayer meeting has solved your vertigo, how can I help you?

I hold up my bottle of Lorazepam.

Me: I need more of this.

She frowns deeply and looks up at me.

Deena: Why are you taking this?

Maybe I should have practised how I was going to answer that question. But I didn't even anticipate her asking it. I didn't think ahead at all, really. I've been focused on step-counting from one day into the next, but even 20,000 steps haven't reduced the churning feeling of needing to get up and move. To outrun this thing that isn't behind or beside me, but inside my head.

My — whatever she is — keeps trying to kill herself.

Her stepmother blames me, even though she won't say it.

I wake up in the middle of the night, crying before I even open my eyes.

I thought I wanted a divorce but actually what I want is for life to stop being so fucking hard.

Putting something back together when you've smashed it like a set of wedding china against the wall is . . . well, it's exactly what it sounds like.

Last night, I ran the water in the bathtub and put on my music loud enough to hear it over the thundering tap and wondered if it would be better to just drive off a cliff than to try to untangle this web.

She looks at me with new concern — alarm, even. I realise it doesn't sound so crazy in my head.

> **Deena:** This isn't normal. And this stuff isn't going to help you. You need an everyday medication.

> **Me:** No.

> **Deena:** Yes. You do. Your anxiety needs to come down, then you can go off.

She's so matter-of-fact. So sure. Probably not a lot of time for bullshit where she comes from, what with all the bombs.

I'd imagined an agonizing drama of pros and cons and advantages and disadvantages and protocols and scenarios, but she just writes me a prescription for Cipralex like it's an antibiotic and I find myself taking the paper from her, disappointed that she's the same as everyone else. So cavalier with medications. If that doesn't work, we'll try another one. Never mind the side effects or the way they can throw you overboard into waves of grief fifty feet high.

Complaint: Anxiety.

Treatment: Cipralex.

How can it be that fucking easy?

"No more than a year. You'll be fine."

Just swallow it.

II: Motivation

In the morning I go in to wake
you up for school, little daughter,
and find you on the floor,
sleeping with your face turned
into the carpet.

You're three.
Weird is your middle name.

Hey. What are you doing?

You turn, bleary-eyed and sweaty.

Your face is green.

What happened?

And you remember
I guess
because you turn your face away,
sharp, quick, like a fox into a hole,
and howl.

What were you trying to be?
The Grinch?

You turn back, full of shame, fear . . . hope
that maybe, possibly,
I will understand?

And where the fuck did you
get a green marker?!

A witch.

A witch?

Jesus, okay.

Well, whatever. Kids do stupid things, and you just have to nod and tell them that next time they should wait for Halloween or whatever. You don't have to fly off the handle and deck them across the face just because that's what your parents did to you.

Deep breaths, one, two, three.

I see. Okay. Well, let's get your face cleaned because today is picture day at preschool.

And I go into the bedroom for my makeup wipes and come back upstairs and the water is running.
Why is it running?
And I turn around and oh, my God, you've got the sink full of water and
What are you doing?

Plunge.
Your uniform
into
the water.

Why?
Stop that!
Yank the tunic out of the water and turn off the tap.
But you're pleased. Smiling.
Proud because . . . because you're three and —
It's all wet. Now I can't go to school.

And the rage, white hot,
starting in my stomach and spreading
like a heat rash through my body
as I stand and stare at you
and the uniform
and your green face,
dripping water on the floor,
on your white shirt.

It's just water.
It's just time.
It's just a moment in water in time
but the rage feels permanent,
dangerous,

And I don't want to feel it because
that's what makes parents hit
their kids and I never want to
do that to you so

That's the day.
that's the day, I . . .
that's the day I take out
the first tiny white pill

And swallow it.

III: Decision

Me: I know I need them, but I am really worried about taking these.

She's sitting in her usual spot, across the very low table and directly in front of the window. She doesn't subscribe to the therapist's triangle, with her seat placed closest to the door in case she needs an escape route. I asked her about that once — what would happen if she had a patient go rogue — and she just said, "I can take them."

Which is why she's been my therapist for years. She can take me. She can sniff out bullshit and hand it back to me on a china plate and make me examine it.

Now she raises her eyebrows and nods like I'm a child who's hit upon the right answer in math after multiple failed attempts.

Counsellor: Perhaps because you've just witnessed someone go into a suicidal death spiral after starting something similar?

Perhaps.

Perhaps because I know what's in them and what they do and I'm not sure I want them to do that.

Counsellor: You went to your doctor for relief from anxiety. What did you expect would happen?

I can't tell if she's chastising me or checking my mental status, but either way, I feel rebuked. What did I think would happen? I thought there would be a magic pill that nobody had tried yet. That maybe I could discover it. Maybe it was mushrooms, after all.

It's not my fault. It's not her fault. It's not anybody's fault but now we're all medicated.

Start with half, Deena told me.

But that half makes the edges of my vision blur and the edges of my thoughts swim. My cousin, who's visiting, looks at me strangely.

I think I'm stoned.

I think you are, too.

I laugh.

IV: Resistance

You're not crazy,

I am,
I *am*

either before or after,
if you're swallowing those
pills, you are.

V: Concession

Swallowing it makes everything numb:

The way your first dad walked out and didn't come back when you waited at the kitchen table in your overalls, waiting, listening to the phone ring. You can see it like you're looking in the window. Feel it in your two-year-old body. Numb those butterflies, that plunging in your stomach, the way your hands and arms and body will shake for the rest of your life whenever anxiety lights down on your brain.

Numb the arguments. The way your wife speaks to you when she's angry. The way your girlfriend flirts with Intent and Plans almost as much as she flirts with you.

Numb it all.

The backhands across your face and the hairbrush hitting your shoulder and the feel of the stairs under your back when you woke up near the bottom with your head ringing, ringing, and you wondered who to call and how to say the words, if they even existed.

It's fine. It's ACE. You're over it.

They're just memories. In the past. Leave the past behind you. Move on. Swallow it.

Suicide Song

The playlist of our life began and ended with "Cleopatra."

Damn your wife, I'd be your mistress, just to have you around.

I'd sing for you even though I didn't sing anymore.
"December," in the car when we were coming home in the twilight,
turning off the main road, down into the country
with no streetlights,
me driving, even though I didn't like driving,
because you didn't like downtown but wouldn't say.

That was before I knew how much you hated being a passenger
and we just tried on this role-reversal first because . . . ? Because.

The music of your life was Pink because the downbeat was perfect for squats
and burpees.
The music of my life was everything I'd left behind from every music room
and stage along the way.

Yes, I miss music like it's an organ that's been severed.
No, I don't want it reattached, thanks.
That never works.

I used to sing along. You pretended not to listen, lips twitching.

But everything is different now. Music soothes the demon howls in your head,
so we keep it on all the time. Not realising quite how loud it needs to be . . .

Suicide is your new cloak that cinches with a lock we don't have the key
for. We can't get it off you; it's smothering you and you're going to have
to live in it until we decipher which combination of pills, psychiatric care,
hospitalisations, therapies, electric shock, and ER visits will set you free.

So far, nothing is working.

So far, we just crank up the volume of distraction and keep pacing the roads.

I finish marking papers while your stepmother runs errands, and you sleep in. You hate to wake up in the morning. If the doctors were able to put you in a coma until they figured out how to flip the switch of your illness back off, you would agree. I would sign the papers.

But the months are wearing on and the two-person tag team your stepmother and I make is no longer enough. Reinforcements are imminent. You need a new special forces squad, and we are about to assemble for the first time.

We will be the A-Team.

> *Every time my car starts*
> *"The A-Team" starts*
> *playing.*

> *I guess I've never downloaded another song that comes*
> *before it in the alphabet.*

> *Some days I crank the volume down before I hear a note*

> *Because . . . because.*

> *But sometimes I like that you say hello.*

Gravel crunches under her tires on your parents' long unpaved driveway. I leave you at the table with your coffee and walk out into the warm and heavy air.

We have missed half of summer. Fall is bringing in its bags. The days have all blended together to form a long, white hallway and I haven't noticed the leaves changing or the turning of the clocks.

Fall reminds me of school.

School reminds me of music.

Music reminds me of loss.

> *And so it now follows that all music reminds me of you.*

Music rooms smell like libraries,
sheet music and leather cases
brimming
like encyclopedias,
and I smell trumpets in the memoir section,

hear strings in lit-fic.

Quarter notes are my favourite perfume.

I used to float so low on the notes of my tuba —
an instrument people love to laugh at, but
love was all I felt for the yards of brass
and the bass notes, vibrating against my legs.

It didn't take much air. Not nearly as much as a flute.
What counts is the embouchure.
Another word that rolls like music.
Like the Latin words to Christmas carols,
sung surrounded by the choir at the church,

Controversially.

Controversy. My first.

We practised the songs but
objected to the
church location for the Carol Service
because
it was a secular school
and church wasn't fair
to the Jews.

In solos,
my voice shot straight to the top
of the apse.

Traitor.

Your friend Natalie gets out of her car and hugs me even though I barely know her. She's shorter than I am but her biceps could crush cans, and when she wraps her arms around me, I almost stop breathing. Relief, maybe.

We walk around your stepmother's garden.

"How much supervision does she need?"

I will get used to her matter-of-fact way of speaking. Her casual bluntness. One day, it will be the thing that calls me back from the brink of the abyss when I want to jump.

"She needs someone with her all the time," I say.

"Can she go to the bathroom by herself, or should she leave the door open?"

I don't answer right away. I haven't been able to bring myself to take away that last aspect of privacy for you and now wonder if I've been wrong. Or really, how many ways I've been wrong. How many mistakes I've made.

"She's okay that way. But we've taken her pills and her car keys."

She lifts her chin, like this is all expected news. I wish I'd called her earlier. But it's hard to find someone who will take a friend's swan dive into mental illness in stride and not ask a million questions or dissolve into tears, making it easier just to do it all yourself.

THIS ISN'T YOUR JOB. YOU HAVE A DAUGHTER TO LOOK AFTER. YOU HAVE YOUR OWN LIFE.

But my daughter is in preschool and very full of life. She does not plan to walk in front of a bus.

Nat and I visit, and I make tea, like it's my house.

It feels like it's my house after months of working at the kitchen table.

I know where every spoon and cup and appliance is kept, probably better than you do, and you live here.

But you don't make the tea.

There have been so many homes. So many new starts. So many abrupt endings and whirlwind beginnings. All I ever need to know is, where do you keep the teaspoons and the kettle?

My father's one-room apartment after the incident at the park and the police at the door.

The new house in Toronto. Then the other new house in Toronto.

Then my stepmother's house, before that incident with her trying to run me over.

Then my grandparents' house.

Then the university dorm.

Then my apartment.

Then my first house. And my next house. And this last house . . .

And now, your stepmother's house, after the incident with you trying to get yourself run over.

That morning, I stood in the doorway and watched you sleeping, like I did to my daughter, wondering what was going through your dreams at that moment — a peacefulness on your face that I never saw while you were awake.

You like it when I sit on the bed with you and read while you're lying with your eyes closed, letting the Lorazepam begin to numb your thoughts. You like it when I take a nap at the same time so you don't feel alone. So you can feel okay about putting your head in my lap and letting the force field down while you sleep. But I can never sleep. I'm always watching out for a sign now. Another lie. Another attempt.

We finish the puzzle, and I glance at the clock. Your stepmother is late.

You see me looking and speak for the first time in an hour.

"You don't have to babysit me. Seriously. My dad will be home in a few minutes. I don't want to hold you guys up."

We ignore you.

I still can't look you in the eye and I don't want you to know that. Trust is palpable and I can't feel it between us anymore. I don't trust you not to take those five minutes alone and turn them to your own dark purposes. And I also know you are terrified of being alone, no matter what you say out loud.

No matter how angry I am at you for looking me in the face and telling me you were going to the hairdresser, then ending up facing down a Mack truck on the highway.

"Hey. Does that bench have any music?" Natalie opens the seat and starts riffling through the pages: hymns and Broadway classics.

I stare without touching, but the music calls to me like old friends through a temporal anomaly and I find it in my hands without remembering having reached for it . . .

"Think of Me."

In the old studio apartment
near Davisville Station
where I took the subway in my
forest green tartan every
Wednesday afternoon,
trudging up to the fifth-floor flat that
seemed more like a solarium than a place
to live, all green plants and chipped white tile
and the bedroom with a piano in it.
Me, alone with the curly-haired
tenor in his favourite black turtlenecks —
the first gay man I ever loved —
bonding over "Memory" because nobody else loved Elaine Paige quite
as much as we did.

He flushed scarlet
when I asked him why he had no bed in his house
and he admitted he didn't sleep there.

Because? Because . . .
He slept at a friend's.

She takes it out of my hands and leafs through it. I know she plays the piano, but the nimble way her fingers dance over the keys surprises me. It's like a siren song, the warm-up. The opening chords. I stand without thinking about it and stretch, breathe, like I'm going to sing.

But I don't sing anymore. I haven't even done scales in years.

Really? Even knowing you were coming here?

My last voice teacher was unimpressed with me. She was good but she wasn't the curly-haired tenor. Nobody was the tenor. And I was an adult then. Too self-conscious to crack in front of someone new.

I told you — organ reattachments never work.

The notes surge from the piano. That warm, blunt quality to Natalie's personality transposes to her playing, too: precise and without apology.

"Ready?"

"No."

But she plays the opening chords again and my vocal cords respond without permission.

No. I don't sing anymore.

A fire ripping through the music room, burning up all the paper and leather, the strings, the wood, the brass. There was nothing left but a pile of ashes.

But you're a phoenix. You'll rise.

No.
Not this time.

Singing with someone is like sleeping with them. Pure entanglement of the physical and emotional, soaring up and down over peaks and plateaus and then beautifully, relentlessly climbing . . .

Natalie grins at me, and I put my hand on her shoulder, laughing out loud as I gear up to the crescendo.

I can't, I can't.

"Come on, you can do it. It's not that high."

"It's *so* fucking high."

"Go!"

She guides me by the melody, and I close my eyes and I know I'm flushing because you're watching me . . .

But oh my God, my voice can still do this. Opening to that note that should be impossible but somehow isn't, then cresting like a wave coming into shore.

For half a second, we're silent.

My chest is ringing, and my ears are hot, and my hands are shaking because singing is like being on a roller coaster with faulty bolts and you never know quite what's going to creak or crack . . .

> *And then life cracked down the middle*
> *and there were all the endings without*
> *goodbyes and all the beginnings*
> *without roots and me . . .*
> *free floating*
>
> *without music.*

"Fuck, that was a hard song." I'm half laughing and half gasping, trying to get in enough oxygen.

"But man, you have a beautiful voice," says Natalie.

"Agreed."

Your voice comes from the couch, low and quiet. Like you've just awoken from sleep. Like you're seeing something for the first time. Maybe me.

I look at you. At *you*, for the first time in days.

Your eyes hold an apology, the same as the note you left.

I'm sorry, I just couldn't fight my demons anymore.

And I breathe into that. Accept it. Sit back down.

Twelve Days on the Psych Ward

Day One

I run into Them in the coffee shop —
the place across town
I've gone to deliberately
so I won't see anyone
we know.
But they're there, sitting in
gossip groups and
caterwauling over
strawberry smoothies.
They ask how you are,
eyes gleaming,
salivating for the scoop.

She's fine.
Not mentioning the plexiglass
that separates you
from the outer hallway
or the way
I watch you through it
while you stare down at your hands
like a kamikaze fish
who might jump the rim
at any second.

Not that you could go far
with that blue gown
tied at the back.
Not yet trusted with clothes.

You're worried you haven't seen
       the doctor.
              Your doctor, any doctor.
It hasn't been your turn.
You haven't been called all day and
you're still in this threadbare gown

And what the hell have you done,
volunteering for this?
Twenty-four hours ago,
you were in the ER again,
head resting on my lap
while I waited for your dad
and you waited in that
l i m i n a l   s p a c e
of too much lorazepam
while the psych resident filled out a
            Safety Contract.

One night on the lye-
washed pillowcases
with halogens
buzzing like mosquitoes
and the guard
posted outside your door, hungry
after his unexpected double shift,
and you've forgotten
            everything.

Maybe that's for the best.

You disappear into the little corner
office to talk about your plans,
and if you had a Plan,
and what
            THE PLAN
is going to be now
for your stay. However long
that might be.

The psychotic in the corner paces
the length of the room,
holding his jeans up with one hand because, well,
No Belts.
And I sit on the cracked vinyl couch
waiting,
dirty lino, crushed board games,
tables bolted to the floor, self-affirmations
pastelled on paper posted

on the wall with tape, because, well,
No Tacks.

I wonder if one of them is yours.

She looks well.

Drugged properly and Safe.
Inside with the room next to the nurses' station,
doctors on call,
far away from large trucks and overpasses.

She should be home soon.

I smile.
Turn away and pretend to work.

Day Two

You're rooming with a woman who stops
in the middle of the hall and
doubles over,
gasping for breath.
Can I help you, my dear?
reaching out your hand to her
while
nobody even blinks,
while
she leans against
the wall,
her face twisted in pain
because
she blew her esophagus out
with
whatever she took.

The doctor in you can't watch
her suffer.
But you're a patient now,
so you have no choice.

Day Three

They buzz me into the main hallway,
not even a gathering spot
but a pedestrian roundabout
where patients come
from every direction,
careful not to collide on their way
to the common room — pudding,
the laundry room — soap, coins,
the nurses' station — cigarettes and cell phones,
like merging
onto a highway at a
dead stop.

But when I leave to get you
a chocolate bar
from the vending machine,
the head nurse chases me
halfway down the hall,
thinking I'm a patient
who's escaped.
I back away, still facing him,
explain about the vending machine
from a safe distance.

Through those fire doors
is the suite where my wife
and I delivered our
daughter.
The smell brings me to the moment
her toothless gums clamped
down on me
for the first time.
No idea that
adjacent to the maternity wing
was the psych ward.

I wonder if they're going to drag me back
behind the
locked doors,
issue me a gown to match yours.

The nurse is tall. Broad-shouldered and built
like he does hours in the weights room
to forget what he sees here.
But he just points the way to the cafeteria.
Retreats.

Inside, it's recreation hour all day.
Reminds me of when we took turns
playing Trivial Pursuit with you, or
            dumped a puzzle on the table
and helped you fit the pieces back together.

The irony lost on no one.

Only here, the other players look like
the cast of *Girl, Interrupted*
and the psychotic with no belt screams
death threats if you look at him
            when he drops trou.

Day Four

You tell me the little one with the hijab
and fragile arms like a bird's wings
is the one they have to hold down
for her shot.

She's a grad student and let go of reality one day —
a balloon too heavy to hold, offered up to the sky
in exchange for days of respite
from her thesis.

In here, she holds the wall to root herself to the floor
and screams when they bring the needle to her arm.

Day Five

Anxiety doesn't feel like worry.
It feels like fire ants.

You're the one who's committed but I'm the one now medicated
for your illness. A daily 10 mg pill my doctor gave me with a glare and a warning
to start as soon as possible.

Five things I can see:
- The greige floor, worn out in the pedestrian roundabout
- The television, its own anchor on the split melamine shelf
- The kid in the corner with his chair pulled up tight to the knees of
  two women. His mother, maybe? A social worker? It looks like an
  intervention. He looks high. Agitated. Up and down off his chair, his
  ungainly long legs springing him up like he has geysers under his
  shoes (The year after you are released, I'll see his face in the paper
  when they recover his body from the river.)
- That flickering lightbulb above the couch that spasms and starts and
  finally dies
- Your eyes, without your glasses on (You only ever used them to read
  patient charts. Here, you're not even allowed to read your own.)

Five things I can smell:
- Hand sanitizer — foam that can't be consumed
- Talcum powder
- A hundred thousand meatloaves etched into the floors, the walls, the
  blinds
- Stale sweat on clothes people have slept in and eaten in and paced
  the floors in, then slept in again
- Feet

Five things I can touch:
- The melamine cup on the table. And the melamine plate. And the
  melamine box we're standing in
- The cold metal chair frame
- Your hand (But I don't.)
- The pencil you asked me to bring
- My sweater that you reach for. The one you like to wear

Five things I can taste:
- My gum
- My saliva
- I don't like this question — I really don't want to taste anything in here, especially not the air

Five things I can hear:
- The voice of that one asshole doctor — some sort of brogue on the edges of his vowels — who talks to that patient like she's an insect instead of someone who just desperately wants a hall pass
- The scraping of chairs
- The buzzing of the door
- The laugh track to a movie that was made before I was born
- In my head, on loop, your voice choking out "I'm not in love with you" the day before you came here to stay

Day Six

I find out you've got grounds privileges and phone your stepmother. She's only
ten years older than you but
she's the wisest and sanest one so we let her play the mother role

~~until it goes to her head.~~

They do know what she tried to do, right?
They're letting her walk alone — right next to the highway?
WHY THE FUCK IS SHE EVEN THERE, THEN?
Why not just hand her the keys to the narcotics safe
or a sharpened scalpel?

Later, when we're walking in the courtyard
you tell me how long
you spent watching the trucks
                                        fly
through the intersection
before finally remembering
that when you signed out
        you also promised to sign back in.

Day Seven

I don't go to see you today.
I let your boyfriend take a turn to sit among the runners
and the screamers.

I imagine him, head down, embarrassed,
            trying to excuse himself but not knowing how,
like that day you missed your plane south because
the voices in your head kept singing songs of doom
and you couldn't shut them up.

            Then he came up to collect you,
only to find you in this new state,
the state where your life was swallowed by that
            word,
the one that everyone whispered but
            wouldn't say out loud,

            especially to you.

And he said he had to leave . . . but none of us can remember why.

Me: How are you feeling?
You: Shitty.
Me: Swear. It helps.
You: FUUUUUUCCCCCCCKKKKKK.
Me: That's better. Goodnight.
You: Goodnight.

Day Eight

You text and say you need something
to do. You don't know what.
Could you even read a book in there?
I don't know.

I go to your flat — our flat?
The flat where you slept and I worked.
The flat that was your refuge after your
divorce,
and after my separation/reconciliation,
when being   not-divorced
was almost harder than just
having gone through with it.
During your decline and
my caregiving. The flat above your clinic
where you built an
attic studio
that nobody used
because you could never bring yourself to give it to me

and I never asked.

I rummage in the drawers you've so recently filled,
remembering the day we moved it all from your house
in the few hours your then-husband was
away,

find a book and a new shirt
even though you rolled your eyes.

There's a laundry machine
but the smell of the place clings to everything,
even my hair when I'm sitting in the bathtub
every night
washing all my thoughts into the bubbles,
blowing away, forgetting,
while Spotify picks something it thinks
will make me
breathe normally.

You're saturated by now.

I hear downstairs, through the thin walls
and stage whisper
of the small-town grapevine, patients coming in
just to *express concern.*
They think you have cancer.
They've gotten together in their small-town cliques
and fretted about your weight loss.
Your divorce.
The woman who works in your office who
you seem *very close* to.

What is happening? We have the right to know.
I walk down the stairs
through the waiting room,
push out the door, ignoring their stares,
enjoying the sound of the air whooshing
over their open mouths,

the whistle over a bottle neck.

And after my wife drops me off
at the hospital
so I don't have to find a place to park,
I hand you the bag
at the picnic table
next to the main doors.

You strip off the old reeking shirt,
sitting in your sports bra for a second
before putting on this threadbare blue thing
that I chose because it looked like
it was almost worn out anyway,
like a week on the psych ward
wouldn't send it spiralling
because it had already
hit rock bottom.

You drink in the smell
of your own fabric softener.

The old Italian men taking their sun
on the metal bolted benches
look at you, brows dancing.

Day Nine

The food they serve you
should send the paranoids flying:
all textures, all flavours
       mixed up
and spat out
before you even have the chance
to gag on it.

When we were Watching you,
it was puzzles and sandwiches,
a walk around the block,
Ativan to end the day.
No spices.
No heat.

Until that one lunch hour
you said you couldn't eat and
       spat out the fajita into a napkin,
then made me call and cancel all your patients.

I should have known then
that
when you hugged me tight
and said you were going
for a haircut . . .
I should have known
that you'd already written the note.

Day Ten

Ten Things I've Learned Since You've Been Here

1. Don't make eye contact with the bald man with the raspy voice who asks you for a light. I don't know why. I don't need to know.
2. Psychiatrists do not specialise in the psyche. They specialise in medicine. Their treatment of choice is drugs.
3. Nobody wants to hear you talk. They don't know whether to trust you and so they would rather you were silent.
4. Drugs make the problem worse before they make it ~~better~~.
5. Depression does not look like sadness.
6. Suicide is not an event. It is a state of being. The outer skin of someone's life. An identity.
7. Sometimes diagnosis is not possible. Instead, you need to find a space among all the overlapping circles of LABELS and put your head down to rest, because this is a very long road.
8. There is no cure for what you have.
9. There is no returning to normal.
10. Normal was just the Before in this new narrative.

Day Eleven

I bring you lunch from home so you remember that there is food in the real
world. That this is a fissure in time. A time warp. An alternate reality that you
could sidestep. You eat your bologna sandwich and mine. All the chips. Give
me back the yogurt with a look. I should know better.

I do, but I'm mad at you and can't be mad at you because you're in here so
I'm punishing you with Activia.

We sit among your friends in the outside gazebo, discussing stimulants
and sedatives and how many they can take while still functioning. It's hot.
September. Out here, in the place between the time warp and the real world,
the seasons are turning, and the leaves are turning, gold and red, and the cars
are turning in the parking lot — light glinting off their windows.

The doctor who committed you walks by and shakes his head like you're a
child who got her way against the rules. He's the one with the brogue. The
one whose contempt leaks through the very lines around his mouth. Like you
relish the destruction of your own life — the sale of your practice, the fallout
of your marriage. The obsessive thoughts that convince you to take on a
Mack truck in your bare feet.

You offer him an apologetic smile
and I want to smack him.

Day Twelve

They alter your medication again.

Brilliant.

The first one made you worse.
The second one made you manic.

But they don't say manic.
Or high.
They say *improved*
and let you out.

I say, "Don't give her the car keys for fuck's sake."

You laugh.

Healing is not linear, darling.

And neither is this story.

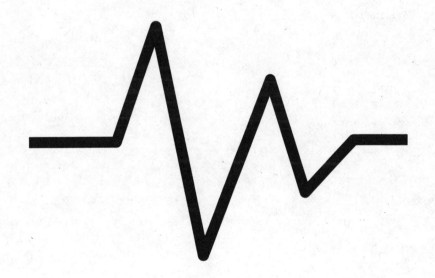

Last Day

"Take a piece of my heart
And make it all your own
So when we are apart,
You'll never be alone."
– Shawn Mendes, "Never Be Alone"

You're moving.
In with the old/new boyfriend
who won't let you hang your artwork
in his house.

You sell your practice and your life.

And as we say goodbye, you hug me as
tight as you did the day you went for a
haircut, and you whisper,
"Love of my life,"
not meeting my eye as I pull away and
step back, heart thudding and eyes
filling and hands shaking because

What?
Now?

When your suitcases are packed and
~~our~~ your apartment is cleared out and
you've given away your dog that you
love so much because the old/new
guy is allergic (and honestly, what the
fuck are you doing with someone who
is allergic to dogs, anyway), and I've
climbed a year's worth of reconciliation
steps because she's a good woman and
a good mother and even though
she & I
couldn't be more different than

you & I
she's my lifeline when I'm yours and
she's the one I married and

marriage is work.

This is work too but **this** is what we're
supposed to let go because
didn't you just, a month ago, stand in
this very same spot, not looking me
in the eye for the first time in our life,
and move away from me and sit frozen
while your stepmother scolded me for
confusing you, then touch my arm as I
went to leave and look at me, holding
your breath while she watched, shaking
her head.

Your eyes full of love and fear and
hope and apology as you put both your
hands on my shoulders like you were
going to hug me and I let you because
I knew you were sitting on a thin sheet
of cracking ice like the day in my office
you first met the monster face to face,

Please don't leave like this.

And follow me outside and
look at me with your words stuck,
stuck, as you walked faster and faster
and I switched sides to keep you out of
the path of traffic and . . .

Time stopped.

You stopped.

I stopped.

And you put your hands up and said, *I
love you to the depths of my soul, but I'm
not in love with you.*

Because you were scared. So scared.
And the ice was cracking and you were
going to drown so I didn't touch you
and didn't slow you down to say, *What
the fuck do you think the difference is,* but
said, *Okay, it's okay you're not, and I'm not
either,* instead of:

*If you were, that would be fine and
I understand and
there's nothing wrong with you and
we will figure it out and
this doesn't change anything and
I love you, too.*

But now?

Now that I'm about to turn around and
walk down the stairs, and nobody's
listening and by the time I could tell
anyone, you'd be on the highway, all
this in the rearview?

Now you choke, "Love of my life" into my
hair and look at the floor and say you're
still going to move in with him?

And you hand me the painting of the
blue heron — the one that used to hang
in my office that you say should stay
with me because . . . because.

You're going. You have to.

I'm staying. I have to.

But these are the last words you're
choosing?

(This, doll, this is the last moment I will
ever see you alive?)

Your move is dangerous. You're leaving your town, the one that runs through your blood like the elements. You're leaving your family, who might not be good at Shirley MacLaine-ing but will at least run toward you. You're leaving your identity. You're leaving your friends. You're leaving your sports, your dog, the Dr. in front of your name . . .

But you're also leaving the rumours, which is the only thing that matters.

I can see the monster stalking you from across the miles. Can tell by the tone of your voice and the length of your texts that he's got you again.

But I can't watch from here. I can't watch you self-destruct after I've tried so hard to hold you together until you could save yourself.

You're drowning and you went into the ocean on purpose so finally . . .

I think this is where we part
ways, my dear. I wish you
nothing but happiness.

Because Christ if it isn't going to kill me to watch you try and build a life with him from all the broken pieces of your past.

And you tell Natalie, "Steph broke up with me."

And she comes to my house and walks with me around the block and up to the cafe and says, *Are you okay*, and I just look at her and she says, *Yeah.*

My move is bigger than your move.
I load my family's stuff into a cross-
country 18-wheeler and find a spot of
land in a special time zone as far away
as possible while still being in Canada.

My backyard is the ocean.

If I step into it, I'm off the edge of the
map.

The salt air stings all the cracks in my
flesh and I welcome the cleanse and the
new start on the red sand where I stand
on the edge of the cliff and watch the
lobster boats on setting day, and life is
dictated by tides and storms and the
will of the Gods.

Nothing is familiar.

Everything is new.

In the winter, the night I graduate
my doctorate, the night before my
grandmother dies, I take the painting
and stuff it in the fireplace, watching
the flames lick it to ash.

I think I've finally left your orbit, not
realising that you aren't the Earth —
you're gravity.

The Acrobats in My Head

Week One

Steph, c'mon. You're supposed to taper. Don't quit cold turkey.

You know that.

You *know* you're not supposed to quit cold turkey, so why did you do it?

Never mind that doctor you saw last year who looked at your dosage of 10 mgs and said that, honestly, at that low a dose, you could just quit. You know better. You've seen what happens. She might be good with whole foods and the raw lifestyle but, Jesus Christ, did she never do a psych rotation? She should perhaps take a stroll down the central hallway of the Royal because maybe then she wouldn't flip the bird at the psychosis that can elbow out good faith and reason at the drop of one tiny pill down the drain.

You've seen it first-hand so why hasn't she?

And yet . . .

On half the dose, you should be fine, right? There's nothing to taper down from when you're already cutting them in half. (But you could take it every second day, then every third day, then stop. You could be easier on yourself. You could practise the *self-care* you remind other people about. You could go slow.)

But once you decide to stop, you don't want another chalky little white half-pill ever crossing your lips again and you think, the only way out is through, and you just stop. taking. them.

You haven't seen her in years — not since she moved in with her old/new boyfriend and you moved to the ocean with the red sand, and now you're done your PhD and you're done single-parenting, and you're done steering the second love of your life away from Mack trucks, so for the love of fuck, why aren't you done with the pills?

You are. You are done. You are so done. You are so done *today*.

The mania hits first: a rare side effect, you're told, but one that grabs you as a dance partner on the first day because you wake up like acrobats are flinging around in your head and you're ready to GO.

Straight to the mall, where you haven't dared to go for the past 235 pandemic days. Three hundred dollars on Christmas ornaments at a dead-quiet Michaels where everyone has to wear a facemask and you're not supposed to linger; but really then *why* do they have these sales with their impossible BOGO choices?

Focus, focus. You don't have ADHD but you feel like you do. You're not on cocaine but you feel like you are. Your bipolar dad is not actually your dad so you can't catch it from him otherwise you might worry because, holy shit, this feels like flying.

You're a rational, non-medical doctor with a degree in psychology and the benefit of eyes-wide-open anticipation and you're still high as a fucking kite after stone-cold turkey dropping your low-dose meds.

But you feel great.

So screw the nausea that's coming down the pike. Screw the vertigo on its heels. Screw the sleeplessness and the lack of appetite and the *fucking migraine* that's clenching your head like a vice because the lights are SO BRIGHT right now. The colour is saturating. You're Dorothy in the moment that colour seeps into Oz.

> **Discontinuation syndrome is characterized by flu-like symptoms, insomnia, nausea, imbalance, sensory disturbances, and hyperarousal. These symptoms usually are mild, last one to two weeks, and are rapidly extinguished with reinstitution of antidepressant medication.**[1]

But yours won't go away because you're not going to reinstitute any medication because you're done with that shit.

The thoughts in your head do not stop for breath on their way out of your mouth. You tell your wife that you know you're not being rational. She agrees but lets you spend your money on a tin sleigh and a matching mailbox for the North Pole anyway because it makes you happy and you haven't been happy for a long time. She accompanies you to the clothing store. She carries your bags to the car and lets you take her out for lunch. Then she asks you if you're finished and you let her drive you home because the vertigo is getting worse, and the lunch is gurgling in your stomach because your body has somehow forgotten how to digest food while your brain is sucking up so much attention.

But she's always taken care of you and that's why you've been married so goddamn long, because she knows when to argue and when to just keep the receipts to return the shit another day . . .

---

1 Antidepressant Discontinuation Syndrome: https://www.aafp.org

The next day, you work. You close your eyes because the pipeline to your creativity has been turned on full blast and you're being deluged with ideas. You don't have a Pensieve so you go for a walk and try to breathe and think and write everything down at the same time. The vertigo is worse when you're standing, but you can't write lying down so you tuck your knees up to your chest and clench your laptop so awkwardly you get massive knots in your neck, but you keep going.

Day three, you rage and scream and bring the house down because what the hell has happened to your life while you were asleep? You've moved to *Prince Edward Island?* Your grandmother has *died?* These dust bunnies under the couch have just been *living here all this time?*

You clean the house for ten hours and your wife packs her things in boxes to return to Ontario because you're a *fucking lunatic.*

And then you fall asleep.

In the morning, she's still there.

You only have one car and it's COVID, for shit's sake, and she didn't leave you when you dragged another woman into your marriage for the better part of a decade so she's not going to leave you now and besides, where the hell is she supposed to go?

You sold your house. You moved to an island. An island with the strictest quarantine restrictions in the world besides New Zealand. You just bought a goat café. Your daughter just started school. *You all agreed.* It's not like you weren't around for the decisions. YOU made the pro and con charts . . . YOU flew down to do the house inspection. YOU were in the hospital room sitting quietly in that horrible, broken, uncomfortable "bed chair" when your grandmother took her final breath. YOU were thinking, feeling, living in the moment, so what the hell is wrong with you?

You both know what's wrong with you, so you apologise, and she cries and you cry and then you see more dust bunnies and you start cleaning again.

Week Two

Everyone's lives are so interesting right now. Their lives and decisions fascinate you.

Chocolate tastes different.

You're reading a book. A *book*. The plot is amazing and the characters are so real. Their story is nuanced and deep, you are falling into it. They start taking each other's clothes off and you feel a hot flush creep up your body and suddenly you remember you have a body too and it used to like sex — sometime in the past? You used to like to come, didn't you?

Somewhere there's a vibrator in your drawer that still has battery life in it, and you turn it on and lie back on the pillow and close your eyes, and o.m.f.g. that feels good.

Somewhere along week two, you ask your wife if she's still attracted to crazy you or did she give up trying to touch you, not because you kept saying no way in hell, but because she's just not that into you, and she looks at you strangely but says of course she is and of course you can try to see if it's still alive. Even though it's one in the morning and she does not have the same insomnia as you do. Even though she'll be paying for this midnight rendezvous for days while your eyes fly open at 5:00 a.m., ready for your moon launch. Even if she's still wary of you after that Day Three disaster.

The vertigo keeps knocking you for six — even though your sister tells you knocked for six is not an expression they use in the Maritimes and everyone looks at you strangely when you say it, you can't think of another phrase.

The dizziness comes and goes.

The headache has stayed.

The insomnia is camped out permanently like an adult child moving home for quarantine: knowing you can't kick it out even if it's on its worst behaviour.

But you keep going because . . . ? Because.

The strangest part is that you know this is your brain chemistry, unaltered. You know this is how you got along for thirty-four years before you ever took a pill. This is you, uncut, unfiltered. How did you not realise how good you felt? How full of *life* you were? How creative and productive and, yes, also edgy and volatile sometimes . . .

How did you not know? Why did you ever let a doctor prescribe that away?

Why did you let *her*, with her insatiable black hole of depression and denial, knock you off your knife edge along the canyon? You were fine. You were never going to fall. She was the one who was going to fall, and you were breaking, trying to keep her from flying.

Speak of the devil.


```
Hey. How's the vertigo?
Feeling any better?

                        It's a seahag.

Deep breaths. You can do it.

                        Thanks, Doctor.

You're welcome, Doctor.
```

Week Three

The energy shifts darker. You realise that underneath all that medication, you're basically just angry.

Week Four

Your seven-year-old looks at you with her hands on her hips and says, "Tired Mummy is much better than Angry Mummy," so you cry and sniff and tell her you're sorry for being such a bitch and then you swallow down the meds and go to bed. The next morning you wake up groggy and hungover and defeated.

And in the afternoon, you go for your regular nap and you cry going to bed because you've loved not going to bed in the middle of the day and you wish you could have that and also not be angry but you can't, so you sleep.

So you take one day on, one day off, one day on, one day — *fuck this shit.*

Flush, flush, flush until they're all gone and then you wait.

Attempt #3

"Set me free, leave me be
I don't want to fall another moment into your gravity."
– Sara Bareilles, "Gravity"

Over the summer, I try to orbit my own life.

You go to the cottage, far away from technology and I just

stop

                    reaching

       out.

I go on socially distant nature walks and take my kid to the park the day the play structures reopen. We walk the beach, gathering shells. We swim. We play. I teach and write and let the blinking light at the back of my mind keep blinking without answering it.

She's fine. *Please let her be fine.* Without checking on you.

Two weeks go by. Three. Maybe you're okay. Maybe you've finally taken flight — maybe, even after the breaking up and the reconciling and all the ways we've tried to say goodbye, maybe you've finally . . .

Where are you?
I miss hearing from you.

Nope.

                Are you okay? I thought you
                were at the cottage.

I was. No. Things have been
really rough.

And so I call you and we press the steam valve and all the fear comes pouring out and we sit with it and I shake my head and put my hand over my eyes and wonder how long this pandemic is going to go on for and how to get you some help.

The cracks in the façade are finally starting to show and . . .

                              Just tell me the truth.

I'm just really lonely out here.

                              Video me.

I can't.

                              You can. I want to see your
                              face. It's been too long.

                    I know we've already broken up, but.

I'm a mess.

                    Maybe we should have had it out instead.

                              I don't give a shit. Let's go.

          You tell me you love him but you seem more despondent,
             depressed, and lonely every time I talk to you . . .

Your face comes into view and I'm shocked, but I smile.

          You keep away, keep to yourself, and stay sad and silent.
             And it absolutely breaks my heart, because . . .

"It's so good to see you."

You smile back, more of a twitching of the lips. "Your hair is long."

"Right? Bohemian enough for you? It's my COVID style."

"Suits you."

And I've never wanted to put my arms around you more than I do at this moment.

I don't know what to do.

Your face is drawn. Your eyes are dark and the lines around your mouth have deepened. You look haunted — there's no other word. The medication has made you puffy and I know you'll be able to see it in my eyes if I let my face fall. So I smile harder than ever.

It's been years. Years since I've seen you. How can it have been years?

"It's so good to see your face."

You smile again — what seems to pass for a smile now.

Why haven't I made you video me before this?

Because it's too painful. Because trying to be "just friends" took all our energy. Because you dropped the everydayness that gave me the right to see your eyes and read their depths.

"You don't need to worry."

"You know I'm going to worry."

"It's been this way for years."

It has been this way for years, but out of sight, I could imagine it differently.

Or maybe it's me, then. I'm off my meds. Everything seems more urgent, brighter, full of nuance. Something seems wrong here, but I also just spent $300 on Christmas decorations because they were so much fun so maybe my judgment is impaired. Maybe I'm the one going off the deep.

"You look sad."

"I am sad."

Breathe. Here we are again. You, me, and a big old paper-wrapped box of truth that only we can open.

"Tell me."

You look away, down. Can you walk through this door with me, after all this time? Have I wrecked your safe space by closing myself out when I needed to see if it would make things better?

But your words descend like weights, finally. Quietly. You remember how to do this.

"I'm sad I have mental illness. I'm sad that he doesn't have the woman he thought he was getting. I'm sad I can't get better." And your voice breaks and you look at me, half-defiant, and I hold your eyes because nothing about this is okay. "There."

> This is the part where normal people cry.
> That break in your voice is trying to make
> space for tears to come. But you never cry.

"Okay. That's a lot."

"It's all day, every day."

"And how are you coping with this?"

"Not well. Fucking COVID. Everything's cancelled. I can't go to the gym; I can't go to art class. I can't go fucking anywhere."

"Except home to bed."

"Exactly. And then I just lie there and think about taking all my pills . . ."

I look at you.

Breathe.

"We've talked about overdosing before. All the things that can go wrong."

"I know. And it's your voice in my head that I've heard all these years telling me not to do it. And I haven't. I can't do that to him, either. What if I didn't get the job done and he had to look after me . . ."

"Can you tell him to lock up your pills, please?"

"No. I don't want him to know."

"You're not talking to him about this?"

You look away again. I thought I'd passed the torch to him — because you wanted me to. But it turns out you've just been holding it yourself all this time.

I sit down and hold the phone closer to my face.

"What happened?"

"I just . . . I just stopped being able to talk to him."

Deep breath out.

"Doll, this is not a safe situation. Okay?"

"I know."

But you're a warrior and you're used to running a Spartan race every year and then leading Bootcamp when you're finished. In the not-too-distant past, you saw forty patients a day and then ran the ridge and lived to climb another ladder. Help is something you've never sought. Only accepted, gratefully, when it arrived, almost too late.

"We need to do something. What are we going to do?"

But you just shake your head and I know you can't cope with telling him. And now that I've seen it, I can't unsee it, no matter what's causing the seeing: you or my meds.

It's probably already too late — you're heading for the pit, but I still try. I call you after you get home from the barn and before my daughter comes home from school. With the time difference, the window is short. Natalie calls during the few hours before your not-quite-husband gets home from work: the hours you spend lying on your bed, thinking/dreaming/planning how to overdose.

I say, *Tell me what you're thinking*. Partly because I want to know how serious your Plan is and partly because I hope that if the words hit the air, they'll evaporate, and you won't need to nurture them anymore.

You rehearse the steps in your mind, over and over: open the medicine cabinet, take out the bottles, count them, mix them together . . .

I listen carefully. Do you know about the anti-emetics you need to take to keep the rest down? You're the doctor — but not that kind. Still, more that kind than I am. I use the doctor in front of my name as a weapon at the end of complaint emails, mostly. And in signoffs to my students who are late handing in their essays.

We make you an appointment with your psychologist and you go. You role-play the conversations you need to have. "When I say I'm having a bad day, I don't mean I'm sad. I mean I want to hurt myself."

Kill myself. Rosy platitudes aren't going to work. Tell him the truth, doll: *I wake up in the morning wanting to be dead.*

You're back on the waiting list for a psychiatrist and you promise me you will never do this again: freefall into the world without a medical CEO to steer the ship. But it's a long wait and the meds are not working and COVID is putting a stranglehold on your life, and you're isolated and lonely and depressed and the days just keep getting darker and darker.

When snow blankets the entire province of Ontario and I know you're going to be stuck inside all day, I feel pulled to you, twin-tethered at the heart as we've always been — even when I was taking medication to numb the feeling and we were both busy moving ever more distant from each other.

```
                              Are you okay? Silently
                              freaking out is my guess.
```

```
God, you know me well.
```

```
                              Can I help?
```

```
I'm just trying to breathe.
```

```
                              Brain hijacked by anxiety?
```

```
Completely.
```

My heart flips and my eyes fill because what the fuck have you done? And what the fuck have I done? You're too far away to help and it's your fault, but it's my fault, too.

```
                              Can you tell him, please, to
                              take you outside?
```

```
I can't.
```

```
                              Close the door then. Sit on
                              the floor. We're going to get
                              through this.
```

I can't call you because my wife is home and you can't pick up because your not-quite-husband is listening, and it's back into the same old pattern of love without a name with an intensity everyone feels and everyone hates but which we've never been able to stop needing.

```
                          Deep breaths: in for seven, out
                          for nine. I'm here with you.
                          You're okay.
```

But I'm not with you. And you're not okay.

In the end, he finds you unconscious beside the note you've written. In the end, he's the one who has to rush you to the ER. Sit with you in the ICU. He's the one who's got to face up to the fact that he didn't know because he didn't ask, because he didn't want to know. And, from my new, different time zone, I wake up in the middle of the night, knowing precisely the moment you are intubated.

I text Natalie and say, "Call him. I need to know if she's in the hospital."

"Why would she be there?"

"I just have a feeling."

She calls and tells me that yes, you're there. And then she says he's going to call me. I'm stunned he's going to call and can only imagine you've made him.

He sounds broken. Shattered, really. And stoic, like the last time. Wanting me to know he's barely hanging on.

Barely hanging on to the cardboard fantasy he holds up in place of the life you actually have.

His pink glasses are cracked and without them he has to see. This isn't temporary. It's chronic. A permanent part of you.

When we get off the phone, I send him a picture of a safe with a keypad.

```
                          When she gets home, lock up the
                          pills.
```

He hopes you won't be on as many when you get out. But there will always be pills. There have been pills since the first time and things are much worse now.

There will never be nothing to lock up in that safe.

What can I do?

He's searching for an action. Men are always searching for an action.

> Make her walk. Early. Drag her out the door at the crack of dawn to greet the sun.

Make her come. (I don't tell him that, but flushed cheeks and tense legs and hips bucking toward a blinding, body-shattering release is what you need. What you've needed for years while you've been faking it.)

> Take her away, even if she doesn't want to go.

Better yet, bring her here. To her one safe spot on Earth. The one she can't talk about.

In my arms.

Eight Things I'm Putting in Your Care Package

> *"It was not your fault, but mine.*
> *And it was your heart on the line.*
> *I really fucked it up this time, didn't I my dear?"*
> — Mumford & Sons, "Little Lion Man"

RAINBOW ZIPPERED POUCH

When you get taken out of your real life and smacked down in the time warp of long white hallways and group therapy, it's easy to scatter. To ooze out of the boundaries of your body and slide under doors where you don't belong. Your things can get disordered: thoughts and pencils. It's good to have a place to put them back. Something that closes. It has to be transparent, I suppose, so they can see inside. It would be better if your skull were transparent, too.

As usual when you get taken away somewhere there's No Contact, I think of ways to pretend we're in the French Resistance and I need to send you secret messages inside the walls of enemy territory. Letting you know I still love you even when you can't love yourself, or trust yourself, or even will yourself to live.

They've come out with a flat-postage box since the last time, and that makes it easier. I can send you things in plain sight — inside jokes to make you smile and treats to fill your mouth so you can't cram it full of pills. Eat the chocolate bars instead and try, please, to come back from the brink where you've been living for so long. The edge you go to whenever we push each other away.

I walk the aisles of the Dollarama, looking for light things. Things that won't weigh down the postage box or your mind. Everything will fit in here.

You will fit in there, like you did before. Don't let that scare you.

It's possible you won't remember everything. Don't let that scare you either.

The last time you were in that psychiatric clinic, your roommate had rank-smelling feet and it made you fucking miserable but you wouldn't say anything. You wouldn't take her shoes out into the hall or ask her to put them in a plastic bag. You just let her keep them in the room and suffered through the horrendous foot odour for weeks because you didn't want to make things "strained."

What the hell are they teaching you in there, if not to stand up for yourself enough to tell someone with foot odour that their shoes are offensive and to please take them the hell out of your living space? What part of you feels you deserve the never-ending sensory assault of toe jam up your nostrils? Or the assault of cold relationships and unfair divorce terms? And frenemies? And people who will never approve of you and don't want to because disapproving of you gives them so much more power? Why do you punish yourself? Your mother is dead — you can stop now.

That's what I'm most afraid of — that you can't tell me when you've had enough. That we've twisted and tempered this lifeline so many times it's become attached and you can't let go, even if it's hurting you. Even if it's grown barbs and is ripping your hands apart, you hang on because you are so afraid you can't swim the swells in your own head without me to yank you back in.

I saw it before you went in the last time: how afraid you were of me, of us, of what people said. They told me, the rest of the A-Team, how hard you cried when you came in from our walk, the last walk before you went in, when you told me you loved me to the depths of your soul, but you were going to live with him.

If it's No Contact, I wonder if it's for the best. Our relationship is a double-edged sword: your biggest crutch and your biggest stressor.

We've tried it before and we were both miserable, but maybe we didn't try hard enough.

I mean, it's only your sanity and my marriage in the balance of this codependent tsunami we've made for our lives — maybe it's worth a second go.

I haven't seen you in three years, but does that make a fucking tick of difference?

I still message you and you send me back emojis and my heart breaks because I know how much you're not saying.

This time, I hope they teach you to speak.

Role-playing, practising living as a person who knows who she is.

HAIR TIES

You're a girl with a mass of curly hair and a not-quite-husband who will
pack you a shaving kit instead of a toiletry bag. You'll need hair ties.
He's a beautiful man. Like all your men. Beautiful and vapid.
Why did we ever think he could be trusted with you?

A NOTEBOOK

Therapy only works if you talk.

We've let you not talk for years now because it's just so goddamned hard for
you, but it's time now. Silence is destroying you. You're drowning in words. I
can't interpret for you anymore, so let's go.

Feel the moments you're constantly outrunning and let them wash over your
brain until the truth reveals itself.

Take this notebook and write things in it and read them back.

It's a real notebook. Not the tiniest of tiny calendars from the takeout place
next door that gives you space for exactly three words — and only if you use
your tiniest handwriting to put Anxious. Tired. Scared.

This one has full pages of lines. Lots of room for anything and everything,
and the one thing you can't say. It's wrapped in fuzzy turquoise material with
a white-and-pink pill on the front cover. *Chill Pill.*

I don't know if it's too cheerful or too glib or if you might look at it and want
to hurl it across the room, but I like the idea of you writing in a book much
more than the idea of the fistful of meds you need to take or want to take, or
want to get off of, or want to take all of . . .

Yes, I'm an English professor. No, that's not good grammar. And no, I don't
give a flying fuck because I'm tired and I haven't slept well since you went
into this place three years ago when I was in a different city, let alone now
that I'm locked in by stay-at-home orders and you're not even going to try
because they're threatening you with ECT and you'd rather die.

I know there will be some days when you're pacing the floors and climbing the walls because there's less than nothing to do in there. That's for then. You like crosswords because you can puzzle them out for days and nobody knows how long it takes you or if you have to erase wrong answers.

Six-letter word for graduate of Wellesley?

That was last day before your first stay. The day they sent us home from the ER and I didn't know what to do with you while we waited for your stepmother to come home so we cracked open a crossword puzzle and tried to solve them all because we thought it mattered.

Alum is the root. Wellesley is a women's college, so it has to be Alumna.

You stared at me, eyebrows up. I felt a flutter in my stomach at having impressed you because shit, even now, I remember what you looked like in your four-inch heels and tight skinny jeans, and you're still one of the most intimidating people I know.

Multicoloured Pens

Blue and black are depressing as fuck and since you hate any pencil crayons that aren't your top-of-the-line artist brand, I'm not even going to try sending you any. Instead, you can draw with multicoloured pens and stop judging yourself and your work because nobody expects drawings made with multicoloured pens to be good. They're just supposed to pass the time.

You might not recall because #Depression but the last time you were in there you made something in art class and spent half an hour criticising it before I finally screamed at you that you were in a psychiatric hospital and the art wasn't supposed to be good for the love of fuck and maybe this was the problem!

If there's time, because I think they should damn well make time, maybe they could teach you how to laugh at yourself. Like, big belly laughing guffaws at your own damn mistakes. Instead of cringing inward and numbing up those murder-hornet stings with booze and pills and brain-killing dance shows, you could look at yourself in the mirror with tears of laughter streaming down your face because that was just such an idiotic thing to do, and can you *fucking believe how funny that is?*

Like when I learned, during the Great Netflix Binge of 2020, that *excited* in English and *excité* en Français were two completely different verbs and I'd been telling all the French people I met how horny I was to be in Paris.

Of course I was absolutely mortified.

And like the woman who accidentally strode buck naked into her kindergartener's Zoom class because she let him walk around with the iPad and accidents happen when parents have to go on with their regular lives and do things like shower — and she was crying — I mean, *crying* with laughter as she told this story to the entire Internet because what the hell else do you do?

One Small Book of Wordsearch

They're easier than the crossword puzzles and you can do them even when you're blitzed out of your mind on the Ativan they feed you like they're Tic Tacs.

And you can probably still do them after the ECT. You might even be able to do them twice, depending on how bad the memory loss is.

A Get-Well Card

Into every life, a little rain must fall.

Jesus H.

What do you send when the entire Louisiana dam has burst?

A Sketchpad

It's from the dollar store. Just use it to doodle on. Sketch the semicolon we agreed on — our code for needing help. Sketch HELP. Sketch a hangman's noose. Sketch anything but the note you wrote.

You know what? Just give this note to your therapist, okay? Tell her it's the DaVinci Code to your brain. Maybe if she'd just sit and have a glass of wine and a game of Uno with you, everything would come pouring out and someone would finally be able to put you back together.

That's what they're there for. Remind them of that.

All Things Can Be True

What if we just called bullshit on the false dichotomies and refused to concede?

If Trump can refuse to concede a presidency, can we not also refuse to concede our lives? Our well-being and our happiness and our authenticity by always picking just one?

Maybe if we could just get a handle on complexity, we'd stop exhausting ourselves so much. Maybe instead of always hitting one wall or another, we could lean into the shades of grey between white and black that make up the blueprint of the world. Maybe we could shut down the voices of the masses judging and criticising and questioning and suggesting and just tune in to nuance . . .

The million emotions between I love you and I want a divorce. The million choices and possibilities of who we are and why we want things.

There are many, many intersections in the land of life and decisions.

And here we are, at the intersection of Love and Expectation.

You and I said vows and stood in my grandparents' living room and exchanged rings even though we already knew, four years into our relationship, that marriage and romance and life were not ever going to be what we expected. We did it all backwards: parenting, losing a child, grieving and crying, buying a house, giving up on getting married because what the hell was the point, then deciding, fuck it, why not? I didn't like my dress much and you fidgeted through the service but the traditional Catholic part of both of us that said we should be married before having children was satisfied with the exchanging of the rings.

And even though we skipped the honeymoon phase when our foster son died, we loved each other with a deep abiding affection that was better, we thought, because it was more honest. The point was always the partnership. The Institution that made our life work: I pushed, you pulled. I cooked, you baked. I broke, you fixed. You did the car thing, and I did the money thing and we worked like a good business runs: shared values and strong healthy workforce.

We're older. Your hair is grey. Mine is going that way. You still bring me tea in bed and insult my cooking and then have to grovel when I flip out and threaten to never cook again. You paint my walls and then patch them and repaint them when I move the artwork 17 times.

I still let you put your favourite craft supplies in the shopping cart even though I know damn well you will *never use them* and we're just basically throwing our money away.

We have a seven-year-old and a should-have-been-summer-house-but-now-Covid-shelter on the ocean in a province at the tip of the Earth.

We decorate the tree in November because the kid wants to and because it's been a shitty year, and why the hell not deck the halls? Mismatched baubles, a snowman ornament crashing, smashing to the floor, a child in tears, bacon and porridge for dinner because everybody likes it.

That's our family. That's the marriage.

Then there's her & me, alone in our shared, dark world. Ten years later, she's been there when I close my eyes, like a hand in the dark. We have our own cave at the bottom of the sea where we can breathe underwater. You don't understand her, but you do understand me and when she's sick and I'm there, you still run me a bath and make dinner because . . .

Why?

Because we've tried it every other way and it doesn't work.

Separation, divorce, screaming, arguing, conceding, repenting.

The only thing left is accepting.

This is who we are now. She is part of me and I'm sorry. I'm sorry that hurts you. I'm sorry that's not what you asked for. I'm sorry. But I can't live without her, and I can't live without you so . . .

Do you still love me?

Of course.

You?

Yeah.

Okay, well then, the show must go on, even with an understudy temporarily in the leading role.

It's 1:00 in the morning and we're both awake and I say to you, "Well . . . should we?" Because it's been a year, but it's also been fifteen years and the medication is only one part of all the ebbs and flows: the periods and pregnancy and breastfeeding and menopause and moving and stomach flus and petty arguments have all played their part too, and we've just accepted it, more or less. There will be years without sex.

The media would be aghast — a *year*? Yes, a year. It's been a *year*, okay? A WHOLE FUCKING YEAR WITHOUT FUCKING and maybe it didn't feel as good as I'd expected after a full year of hiatus, and maybe my brain is still saturated with chemical castrators, but it was a start.

It was my hands on you and your mouth on me and it was a bridge. A bridge to the next stage, a bridge to the future.

It's not a perfect future. It's not a perfect past. It's not a perfect relationship, but we're learning. Fifteen years in and we're no longer 22 and 34; we're 37 and 49 and we know love doesn't come in bouquets of red roses. In fact, if you ever bought me a bouquet of red roses, I'd beat you over the head with it because, Jesus, all the things we could have bought at Dollarama.

We're learning that relationships are complicated. But they're not complicated because of life; they're complicated because *the things we expected* and *the way things are* do not line up. If we took things as they came instead of constantly trying to shove them into pre-set boxes, maybe we could spend more time walking in the woods holding hands.

We're learning we're not exempt from gender roles because we're queer. In fact, apologies to the entire Alternative movement, but yes, sometimes having two women in a relationship makes things harder. Having two mothers makes mothering murky.

Reject stereotypes! Reject the status quo!

Okay, yes, we're trying but someone has to cook dinner, and someone has to pay the bills, and someone has to do the laundry, and sometimes it's really not clear which of us should be doing it, okay? Because there were no lesbian moms on *Full House*.

You sling the power tools and the heavy stuff, but your mother stayed home and somehow you think you should, too. I birthed the kid and breastfed her and have the Big Job because my mother worked and I thought I should, too, but I don't want to wear the pants in this family overtop of my C-Section scar.

That's complicated. That's not what we expected. But that's also Life.

I never wanted to be the '50s dad, but here I am.

Um, what — you're never going back to work?

No.

And that bomb rolled around in the centre of the marriage for a few years before we figured out how to defuse it. You, in the kitchen, baking cinnamon buns and packing lunches while I stressed over bills and how to make more money while still being in graduate school full-time.

This is what I've decided. I'm a stay-at-home mom at heart and I'm sorry that stresses you out. I'm sorry that's not what you asked for. I'm sorry. But I can't go back to work, even if you say you're leaving me.

Right.

Maybe we should just stop expecting normal.

There is no such thing.

There is no such thing as a normal marriage.

There isn't even such thing as a normal relationship.

Sit here in this café with me and watch. Better yet, when people come in, steal their phones and let's have a quick look at their secrets, shall we?

Oh! Lo! Here we find . . .

There are single people; there are unmarried couples; there are couples with lovers — both secret and open — there are throuples; there are polycules; and there are midnight threesomes who go back to being single people or couples with lovers . . .

There are people who prefer to be alone and have their lovers delivered to their door like a takeaway pizza. They're fine.

There are people who married for love or money or status or sex and have been together years, each in love with someone else. They're also fine.

There are people who've been married and divorced multiple times, looking for something they haven't found yet, and maybe they find it on the third or fourth try, and they are fine.

There are people who are queer and are happy in straight relationships, sometimes with another lover somewhere in the wings, and everyone is fine.

There are people who are queer and are in queer relationships and bring baggage from straight relationships and lots of family drama, and they are fine.

There are people who realise that one person cannot be everything. They are realists. They are fine.

There are unicycles and bicycles and tricycles and four-wheelers.

I am a tricycle. I need both of them to propel me forward. A stable axle and a rear handle that reaches for the clouds. One is my anchor, and one is my muse. You need a lesbian adaptation of a '50s marriage and a husband who brings home the bacon.

For better or for worse looks like this.

Spouses are sometimes not soulmates and soulmates are sometimes not spouses, and that's hard.

That's not what we expected. We've both cried and raged and apologised and then hurt each other again because we thought we had to fit into a box and there was no way out but in.

But there's room for it all if you just breathe and talk and stay honest.

There's room for everything if we decide there is.

This has been a hard-won battle for us. I didn't know how to exist as a bicycle and you didn't know how to be married to a tricycle, and fair game to us both.

She didn't know what the fuck a tricycle was or why she needed a woman in the first place, and even though she has straight privilege and the luxury of running away from the mess we made, I still think she's paid a higher price than any of us.

Because she never saw the box as an option — only a prison.

Doll, I wish I'd learned that earlier so I could have shared it with you while we were still in orbit.

I can need a wife and also need you. I can refuse to put a label on you because there isn't one. I can be a contented wife and a good mother and still be fiercely attracted to everything in you that isn't in her.

You can love him, and also love me.

Love is a sliding scale and so is sex and that means you can be straight if you want, and still need me to hold you tight enough that you can finally exhale, even if you don't ever want anyone to see or to know.

That can be the place you go to in your mind when you're trying to shut that goddamn treadmill off in your brain and just fucking go to sleep, even as he's lying next to you, taking up all the oxygen that you'll give him.

Even when he's standing on the dock, half-buried in his work and his third beer and you still think he's cute, but his presence and the pressure makes you so anxious that you call me to drive two hours up to cottage country to save you from the swirling thoughts in your own head.

Because you want to share your life with him; you just don't want to share your heart.

I understand. I know. Just breathe into it and lean into it and . . . it's okay.

You can want to hold my hand and also be terrified of holding my hand, and then go back to wanting to again. Both things can be true. All things can be true.

You can be a low-voiced, swaggering, soft butch with a phallic car and a love of dogs and horses who wears high-heeled boots and pink lace thongs while shopping for perfume.

You can shiver when I touch you, and, at the same time, fear what would happen if we ever crossed the line. You can want me to make you come and run halfway across the country to make sure that never happens. You can choose never to tell me, but still think it as loud and clear as you want and know it's okay.

You're okay. You're perfect.

Don't let anyone shame you. Don't run just because the pitchforks scare you. They won't use them — they just want you to know they were on sale.

Life doesn't line up in neat columns, left and right. Life is a giant Jackson Pollock painting with shit thrown at it from every angle, and it's still a beautiful, disastrous mess and you can be a beautiful, disastrous mess and still be loved.

All things can be true. All the paint can stick.

Hey. You. I know you can't reach back right now but I want you to know something. This is a special kind of hell, but you are stronger than you feel, and you will survive this. In case there's any doubt:

10. Your illness is not your fault.

9. Falling into the abyss does not make you weak.

8. Planning to end your life does not make us love you less.

7. Talking about your illness has made you stronger.

6. You have been fighting like a fucking superhero for as long as you could and nobody on the planet could beat back this seahag of depression without an army.

5. You're still a rock star and nothing is going to change that.

4. I love you to the ends of the earth.

3. I'm right here beside you.

2. You will get better.

1. Just breathing is enough.

Thirty-Two Days in Purgatory

Day Nine

(Because you spent Days One to Eight on a medical floor.)

Your not-quite-husband texts me to say you're not feeling in the "corresponding mood" but you "appreciate encouragement by texts."

I press my tongue into my cheek and thank him for his insight while simultaneously fantasizing about shoving his mansplaining ass out into moving traffic . . .

I'm sorry. I really am. I know I'm a terrible person but *honest to fucking God.*

She's not in the corresponding mood.

Thanks, yeah. She's not in the living mood either but we're not giving her much of an option, are we?

I text you encouraging memes and wait for you to log on to see them. You respond with broken hearts, which I know from past experience means you're at about a 1.5, with zero being catatonic and 10 being a manic shopping spree with an unlimited credit card. But I keep sending them and you keep reading them and then finally, one day . . .

> Morning, doll. How are you feeling?

. . .

. . .

Fucking shitty.

You've moved from a 1 to a 2. You're at least talking, even if your next words are,

I just want to be dead already.

My stomach drops out and I close my eyes, but I know your body, and I know your brain, and I've seen the ebb and flow of your morning suicide wishes to your night-time rallies, and I've read the *Healing Is Not Linear* mantra so many times that I can write back . . .

> I'm really glad you said that
> because sometimes
> feelings like that just need to
> hit the air.

And then, like a swollen cyst that's been pierced with a tiny hole, your pain comes dripping out — too slow to provide any relief, but at least it's draining a tiny bit, and not growing under your skin.

> It's 24/7 with no relief.
> I can't see past the darkness
> anymore.

And I text you back and ask about the ECT and make coffee for people who come in my door because it's COVID and we own a café now, because why wouldn't we start a business in a pandemic? And I ring them through with a smile and a "Thanks for coming," and then read your words and breathe through them, like I'm telling you to do, and text you back and put out brownies and sweep the floor and make more coffee while I wait for you to type.

It's slow and it's heartbreaking, but it's pages of text, all day long — tiny bits and pieces, individual pixels of the whole awful picture — and I'm keeping you company and feel like I'm beside you in some way.

> I'm exhausted but I can't
> sleep.
> I wish you were here.

The customers clear out, and I clean the place up and go home.

In my own house, the living room is chaos, and my daughter is upstairs playing while my wife is on the couch, nursing an injured foot, so I go straight through to the kitchen and start making dinner.

I chop the onions and mince the garlic and pour the olive oil into the pan for the risotto I am making because it gives me more time alone in the kitchen.

                    Do you have a roommate?

She's coming later tonight.
I hope she's not as sick and
unmotivated as me. Someone like
you would be awesome.

                    Ha! Imagine! I could check in
                    for a few days and we'd run the
                    place. The psych ward would be
                    100x better together.

You send me an lol and my eyes fill up with tears.

I open the fridge door and cry into the milk. Just thirty seconds of tears. This house doesn't have a clawfoot tub like the other one. I can't sit with the water running and music on.

Now I have to blame the onions for my red and dripping nose.

                    Tell me life isn't far less of
                    a black hole when we can talk
                    15 times a day? How did you
                    ever go a week of your life
                    without me?

Not well, obviously.

                    I miss you a lot.

I miss you, too.

I have to sit down for that one. The tears won't stop.

Seven o'clock and you're back to yourself and I can send you links to songs and some virtual games to pass the time and ask you what kind of book you want me to send in the post.

I tuck my daughter into bed and kiss her goodnight. She wants me to lie with her, but she has school in the morning, and I want her to go to sleep and I don't want to leave you alone, so I let her play some music and tell myself she'll be asleep in five seconds.

You send me emojis with tongues sticking out and I tell you about vibrators disguised as lipstick and you laugh, and I tell you I'm done with my meds and you ask me if I'm doing okay this time because remember the #acrobats!?

We talk about your room and the wing and the common room with its nonstop sports on TV and the COVID lockdown.

```
No décor and everything is
nailed down.
```

```
                              Omg.
```

```
Dinner's at 4:30 so you're
starving by bed. Snack time
is at 8:00.
```

```
                    Oh, so you're essentially at
                    sleepaway camp.
```

```
Kind of.
```

```
                    Only with ECT instead of
                    canoeing.
```

```
Lol, yep.
```

This is the most time we've spent together in the past three years. I look at the clock and see it's getting late. My mornings start at 5:00, which is 4:00 for you, so it's bedtime for me, but I don't want to let you go because tomorrow we'll have to start all over again.

```
                    Hey. When you wake up tomorrow
                    and feel like shit, can you
                    remember that by nighttime,
                    you'll feel at least one point
                    better?
```

```
I'll try. I have ECT tomorrow
so we'll see.
```

I wonder how much of your memory you'll lose.

What will your brain keep and what will it choose to wash away?

Maybe ECT will do all the work for you, and you won't have to answer my question: would you opt out?

Maybe you'll lose the memory of our first meeting and everything after.

Zap — erase that day when I came through your clinic door wearing my Ottawa U sweatshirt and dark jeans and our eyes met and I knew you instantly.

Zap — erase the way your hands on my body were so practised and gentle and precise as you cracked and twisted me back together.

Sometimes I feel like I'm doing the same thing with your mind.

Will you remember how much we used to laugh? Will the nighttime rob you of this balance? This normalcy? Will we ever be able to put you & me in a box with the proper label on it? Will it ever stop mattering?

In the middle of the night, I wake up and a letter to you is fully composed in my head.

Since you're there in a safe space, let's talk.

Take me to therapy with you if you like. Tell her everything and let her sort it out for you.

Tell her that talking about your feelings is not just difficult for you — it's almost paralyzing. Tell her your parents never made it okay for you to express anger and fear and failure.

Tell her you need an interpreter in life and that women are safer for you and that scares you.

I'll Zoom in because fucking COVID and fucking lockdown and fucking everything that made you almost disappear.

Tell her. I'll be there.

```
          Keep breathing, doll. Even if
          it just makes you angry. Or
          throw all your clothes at the
          wall — whatever works.
```

113

You go dark after snack, and I wonder if you've finally lost it. Is this what they're trying to drive you to, with 24/7 lockdown? You haven't committed a crime. They took the *committed* part out of suicide — now they say *died by* suicide, did you know that?

You don't deserve solitary confinement. If you finally went postal and started screaming and tossing your cell, I wouldn't blame you. Maybe they came in and sedated you and now you're sleeping off the second treatment and tomorrow we can start again.

Natalie called at eleven and asked why I sounded like shit. I laughed and told her I was a mirror of you, obviously. Hadn't that always been the way? You gesture and I interpret. You careen in for a crash and I break your fall. You spiral down into the pit and I go too deep just to keep you company.

I thought we resolved this. You moved away. I moved away. There are 1,844 km between us. We both did that on purpose — maybe me even more than you. You told me you weren't in love with me. You said you wanted him instead.

So here we are.

My aunt in New Zealand is awake when I get up at 4:00, having given up on sleep for the night. She's developed an almighty twang from 35 years overseas, and when she types "eh," I hear the Kiwi accent photobombing the Canadian expression.

"Why are you off your meds?"

"Because I don't need them. My demons were fine on their own until hers came back out to play. I only need anxiety meds when she's trying to kill herself."

"Yeah. Right. I see."

And when she says, "Yeah. Right," it's not sarcastic, because she's a New Zealander now.

It's 5:45 in Ontario and you're probably dead asleep. And if you're not, you're wishing you were dead so you could be asleep.

```
I hate this place. I'm so sick
and lonely.
```

```
                              Will you just let me call you,
                              please?
```

I let out a breath of relief when I finally hear your voice, even if you're half-blitzed on leftover anaesthetic from the ECT.

You ask me what's happening in COVID today and listen to me talk about lockdown and being stuck on an island — of all the things to say to you when you're locked down in a psych ward on a Form 1 and kept on a Form 3 and handed a Form 30 and Jesus H. — but the pattern of our conversations has always swung from sarcastic observations to soul-crushing commiseration, and why not tell you that life outside the COVID bubble has its own challenges? That being stuck on an island in the middle of winter, surrounded by nor'easters and snow is not as rosy as the rest of Canada seems to think it is, even if that sounds ungrateful.

You're lucid enough to figure out he didn't tell me the whole story.

"No, he didn't. And you don't have to, either."

"No, I want to."

I don't want to hear what happened. I don't want to imagine you lying in the dark, barely breathing. I don't want to see it all in my head: the paramedics rushing in, loading you onto a gurney, down the stairs of that stupid multi-level house you hate, out to the ambulance. I can see your face, eyes closed with the intubation tube in.

But you tell me, and I let the tears gather in my chest instead of down my face.

And I'm livid that he thinks he has the right to keep that to himself — but why should I be angry? He barely knows me, and I expect him to describe how he came home from work and couldn't wake you up and found your empty bottles and your note? Does he know how much you told me and kept from him? Does he even know we talk? Do you keep that from him too?

He has an entire queer subplot playing out under his Catholic nose and maybe he's angry, too.

Join the line, my friend. This isn't what any of us asked for.

Day Thirteen

Go have a shower.

Honestly, I could really use a
shower.

Well, I didn't want to say
anything but
I can kinda smell you from
here, so . . .

Fine. I'm going to have a
shower.

I fully support that. So will
your doctor, I'm sure.
Tell me when you're back from
psych.

And please, PLEASE tell him that this obsessive loop will not shut off and
that you need them to deal with it. TELL HIM THAT TODAY.

Day Fourteen

You text to ask if you can call and I am stunned to hear your voice on the line sounding almost normal. Hopeful, even. The psychiatrist wasn't a total prick. He seemed to get it.

"I told him about the obsession, and he prescribed me Zyprexa or something for intrusive thoughts. They said I could do some of this as an outpatient."

I'm glad you can't see my face when you say that . . .

"Okay. You want me to write this down?"

"Well, otherwise I'll never remember tomorrow."

"Right, brain zap."

"Exactly."

Day Fifteen

                                    In case I haven't told you
                                    today, I'm very glad you are
                                    still alive. Though you can
                                    feel free to keep telling me
                                    how pissed off you are about
                                    it. I get it.

And I do.

Somewhere between four and five a.m., I begin to wonder how I would feel if everyone was trying to keep me alive to live a life I didn't want.

It's clear to me now that you don't want it.

I imagine your team assembled: the A-Team, your partner, your doctors, all discussing your discharge and your Safety Plan, and I wonder if I'd have the courage to slam my hand down on the desk and say, "No. No, I don't think this Safety Contract is a good idea. No, I don't think we should keep forcing her to live an agonizing life. No, I don't think there's a purpose to life for the sake of it."

I imagine their faces — their incredulity and their anger because what the hell am I talking about after five years of trying to keep your head above water? But I'm serious.

I believe in an escape hatch.

What if we let you go?

Like I let my daughter come home from school when she's tired or the class is just too damn noisy. She calls, I pick her up. Simple, easy — the door is always open.

You want to die? Fine. Call me, I'll come pick you up.

                          God, I wish I'd said this.

No, I won't be quiet. I'm not being irresponsible; I'm being realistic.

If it's too much: if the pain is unbearable and pervasive and heavy, why would you want to live? If the loop in your head is a constant, torturous howl, why wouldn't you want to turn it off? If the days of loneliness make you feel like there are nails dragging down your arms, and you're constantly holding in a scream, Jesus H., let's get up from this roundtable discussion on relapse rates and talk about her choices.

Sorry, no, I don't want to hear from you people about the pros and cons of ECT today. We all know the facts. We've watched the videos from the head of psychiatry and read the statistics on recovery. We've been in rooms across desks from therapists and doctors and pharmacists. It's been four years of this unrelenting hell with minutes and hours and days of struggle, so just stop.

Ask her.

Ask her like she has cancer or any other incurable, painful, debilitating disease that medicine hasn't figured out how to treat.

She's told us. She's said it out loud to every one of us:

I want to die.

Can't you see how ignoring her deepest, darkest wish is just alienating her more? You're silencing her with your optimism. Let her speak. Stand with her. If she wants to die, you can't force her to stop wanting that.

Don't look at me that way — she deserves to know. She's an adult. She's a doctor, for the love of Christ — give her some autonomy over her own life. It doesn't mean she'll use it — or maybe she will and all that will mean is that her body won't have to endure the battering of 240 pills and an intubation trach.

Excuse me? Can you pull up the criteria, please? Yes. I want to see it.

- **Serious and incurable illness?** Check.
- **Enduring physical or psychological suffering that is intolerable?** Check.

Print those forms off, please.

How would it work?

Pick the day.

We'll all gather.

We can say goodbye.

And you'll know that this time, it will be successful. You don't ever again have to choose bottles of pills and total isolation. You don't ever have to die alone again.

I think all this late at night, in that liminal space where the impossible seems possible to say. And then, days later, something you say, the tone of your voice, makes me say it out loud.

"I can't do this. I can't do two months here, Steph."

I wait a beat, for once not rushing in to fill the space with reassurance but just . . . stopping.

Breathe and accept.

"I can't believe I didn't get the job done. I just want to die."

"I hear you."

Silence.

Breathe. Accept.

If I say it to you . . . if I talk about that escape hatch . . . if I stop cheerleading. What will happen?

I've been your lifeline for so long that I don't know how to let go of the rope.

Breathe.

"You know I don't believe in life for the sake of life."

There it is — that shift between us when we go somewhere new. When we shine a light on something that's been kept festering in the dark. Your breathing changes. I can hear the calm in you.

I'm surprised by how steadily I can say it. "If you had cancer; if you had a terminal illness and you were in this much pain, I would understand. I would let you go. I wouldn't force you to be here."

Breathe. Accept.

"But I don't think we're there yet."

And the relief in your voice is a timbre I haven't heard in a long time. "But what if we are? What else is there? I've tried every drug. ECT isn't working . . ."

Put it down, doll. Neither of us has to hold this.

And the doctor's voice comes back to me. **Most effective in the second half of treatments.**

I wish I'd let you talk. I wish I'd let you walk through that door I opened. I wish I'd realised here, in this moment, that it was all impossible.

But in this moment, I still have hope, so I say,

"Can we give it more time?"

Day Sixteen

One of these days,
the fog is going to lift,
the air is going to smell
fresh again.
Your heart is going to return
to your body.
You are going to feel
joy.
We will drink a lot
and stay up all night talking
in New York, like we
were supposed to.
You will learn how to cry
and remember
how to laugh,
and life will be
very different.

That's the dream.

Day Seventeen and you still don't want to video chat, but your brain is spinning so I break out the Brain Busters and the Listography and the colouring books and we audio until you get interrupted by the resident psychiatrist and the lunch tray and the nagging, overwhelming feeling of doom, and you forget to call back.

List all your past lovers.

Never mind — I know all your past lovers. Let's go with:

List all your favourite TV shows.

I know all those too but I think TV shows are a safer vehicle for conversation than your ex-husband, or that prick you used to date, or the boyfriend who had a brain aneurysm in his twenties, whose parents put you through hell by taking him home to live in a permanent vegetative state, or the man you're currently living with in this life you tried to permanently escape from, so we talk about ER and Grey's and the history of medical dramas and you tell me about cartoons on weekend mornings when you were young, and I almost hear a smile but you're too far down the hole.

```
At least the treatments give me
something to do. Can you say
desperate?
```

```
                        You're fucking dark, you know
                        that?
```

Day Eighteen

Yesterday, I wrote a letter to your stepmother. I'm sorry. I'm so sorry, but I told her all your secrets. You can't help yourself and you need us all again to help you.

She wrote back that she would put together a plan with your dad.

So here we are, despite the way we left things.

No, you don't need to know what she said to me years ago, when we fell out. Trust me, you don't want to know. You'd never look at her the same again and you need her. She's not a homophobe, she just prefers things to be easy. And not in her backyard.

It was easier for her if you left with him.

It was easier for me, too.

I thought.

You thought.

Anyway, it doesn't matter now what happened back then.

The A-Team is reassembled.

Day Nineteen

When you die,

I will have the semicolon tattoo

put on my wrist

so I can remember you daily. Or on the nape

of my neck. So I

can forget.

;

Day Twenty is when you finally snap. It's been three weeks since you were outside; three weeks since you felt any fresh air or breathed in the moonlight. I don't know how anyone is expected to get well by being in psychiatric jail but that's where you are and there isn't a goddamn thing I can do about it except provide "encouragement by texts."

> You'll get there, a little bit
> more each day.

But you're having none of this shit. You just want someone else to hurt like you do.

> Whatever.

Good. We're finally here then? Fine. Game, set, and match, my dear. It's about fucking time.

> You're angry?

> You think?

If anger were something you'd ever been allowed to feel, maybe it wouldn't burn like such a hot potato in the pit of your stomach but when you throw it, I catch it and hurl it back to you.

> Go ahead, get it out.

You're not used to that. Anger has been your shield and you thought as soon as you used it, everyone would back off, but that's not the way we roll — did you forget? I live on rage.

> I want to hear it. Let it go.

And you let go a string of text-screams that I'm sure feel about as full of release as a limp dick.

> Weak. Try harder.

And you do and I push you again while remembering your stepmother's advice to *keep it light* and thinking, seriously, how *absurd* that is, because this monster in your head is the heavyweight champion of psychiatric illness, isn't he? He's a beast trying to kill you, and somebody's got to bring the thunder to your door and make you fight back. Letting you off the hook hasn't done a single fucking thing.

Now use your words. Why are you so angry?

I'm alive and stuck in this hell hole.

What else?

That's all . . .

I don't think so. There's a lot more you're angry about.

But anger to you must feel about as unbearable as lust and pleasure because you cram it down the pipe. Try to swallow it. But I'm not going to let you do that. I'm going to drag this motherfucking trauma over the coals and make it scream.

You want to punch through a wall? Fine. I'm down with that. What I'm not down with is you carrying all this shit that has nothing to do with you. Quit keeping it all in. Throw it all at the wall. I'm listening.

Trying.

And I know you are. I can feel how shaky you are. How much this conversation alone makes you want to pull the escape hatch on your own life because, Jesus, if this isn't exactly what you were trying to get away from with those pills and that Plan, *but nobody in here is talking to you.* Group therapy is a joke. There are no psychologists in this psych hospital, and your psychiatrist has just asked you if you plan to stay for the whole programme like this is the fucking YMCA. You need someone to take you out to a rage room and let you smash an entire house full of antiques.

But I'm in my living room off the map so we have to rely on the safety net we've built over the past ten (yes *ten*) years and hope that, even with all the holes we've wrenched into it, it will still catch you.

> I know you haven't felt safe in
> a very long time but you are
> now, in this moment. It's just
> us. There is nothing you can
> say that will make me love you
> less, so please, take a deep
> breath and tell me what you're
> wrestling with.

And there's that blistering pimple finally rising to the surface . . .

Death, and how badly I want it.

There.

He hasn't shrunk at all. Or gone away. That demon is still lurking over your shoulder, feeding on your soul. He's attached to you, whispering to you until you promise to let him have his way. You're three weeks in and as suicidal as ever. And worse, everyone's telling you you're so much better.

But you don't want to be better. You want to be dead.

```
I am so sorry. Your life must
have been so sad and so scary
and so lonely to have brought
you to this place.

But it will not be this way
forever.

If I were there right now, I'd
put my arms around you tight
and rock you and let you cry.
```

Hope Acres

"Don't stop trying to find me here amidst the chaos.
Though I know it's blinding, there's a way out.
Say out loud: we will not give up on love now."
— Sara Bareilles, "Orpheus"

It's the same as the last time, only a different man. A different weight. A different set of secrets, but really, always the same one. A different hospital, but the same long halls and the same white walls and the same circle of chairs in the middle of a room and a nurses' station enclosed in plexiglass.

Only this time, we're separated by half a country and a virus that's holding everyone hostage.

The only way I can help you is if you call me, and you have been. Every day. I keep my phone at my side while I'm teaching, while I'm working, while I'm driving my daughter up the red dirt road to her elementary school on rural Prince Edward Island. Always in your orbit.

You're my lifeline right now, Steph.

I know, I'm here.

The sky is heavy with winter rain: an almost charcoal colour in midday. I feel the bands of a headache closing around my eyes but sit on the floor next to my bed, listening to what you're trying to finally tell me.

Nothing is perfect. Pretending otherwise is just exhausting, doll.

I know.

"So, what is it? What went wrong?"

"I fucking hate my life."

Not just a crack in the armour, but a throwing down of the gauntlet. Yeah. I'm not surprised. What the hell did you think was going to happen when you burned all your bridges without leaving yourself even an old worn pathway to get back home?

"I can see that, yeah. Is it him? Is it the house?"

Your voice is low and sad. "It doesn't feel like home."

And I'm not angry or vindicated — I'm just so sad for you because home is the one thing you've been looking for your whole life. A safe spot that was yours alone.

"What part? The relationship or the space?"

Silence.

"All of it?"

Silence.

"Hey. Is that hard to say?"

"It's hard to admit."

"Okay."

"Because I don't know what to do now."

You know, because you've known since you left, that there is no such thing as home anymore.

So what do we do now? You have no safe spaces left in your head. Nowhere to land when you're exhausted from flying. And if you hate your fucking life but can't imagine anything better, what motivation do you have to keep living?

Hey.

Can you dream with me, like we used to?

Can we make you a safe space, not with paint and textiles, but out of thin air?

In our lifetime marathon of chess, I always make the first move.

You're lost. But I don't know where to look for you, or where you want to go. You're stuck in the past, wanting back what you threw away and scorched.

What if . . .

```
              Okay. Well, you're not the only
              one who sometimes wonders WTF
              they've done with their life,
              so I'll go first. I'd want a
              farmhouse on the ocean, lots of
              orchards and a full complement
              of animals. A flat in Paris so
```

```
                            I could see every inch of the
                            Louvre over several years. Lots
                            of time for paint and piano.
                            And you next door.

That could be fun.

                            What part?


All of it. I would look
after the animals.
```

And I stare at the screen for a long moment. `I would look after the`
`animals.`

Why am I crying? Why do I lean my elbows on the counter, and bow down almost double with tears pooling and this ache in my stomach that feels like I'm being strangled from the inside?

Because it hasn't gone away at all.

Absolutely nothing has changed.

Except now you're in a psych ward on lockdown and I'm not sure you're going to make it this time.

But I don't have time to cry because this is serious. It's life and death, this dreamworld we're making. Maybe it always has been. Our lifeline is invisible, but it's the only thing anchoring you to me and me to the solid ground.

```
                            When you start to feel like
                            you're going off the rails, go
                            to the farmhouse in your mind.
                            We'll call it Hope Acres.
```

This is the new thread. We pick it up and add to it. Yet another shorthand, another imaginary life.

```
                            Feel free to populate it with
                            goats and dogs. Hell, have an
                            elephant if you want. You're the
                            one looking after the animals.


Don't forget the horses.
```

Deep breath. Cry later. There isn't time right now.

Obviously there would be dogs and horses. They are your reason for living. Or they used to be. Because in your new life: no dogs. But I don't have to pick up dog hair on an imaginary farm or shovel horse shit, so . . .

```
                    Have ten. This is your future.
```

You're in the garden, where you love to be
the sun on your head making your curly hair bounce higher
the sky blue and clear
        the lavender between your fingers releasing
its South of France scent all over your hands,
but you know
the feeling won't last.

Birds always come.

They fly at you, dive-bombing from the sky, screeching and howling.
Why do   they flock to you? Why
won't they leave you alone when all you fucking want to do
is cut some roses for the table?

Stop. I know you can't imagine it but
stop.
Stand still. Just . . .
let them land.
        Don't scream. Shhh.
Stand still. Stand still.
Close your eyes and breathe.

There. They've landed.

Now, just wait.
No, they won't bite your ear or peck your eyes out.
        They only want to be heard.
To make you feel the weight of them on your shoulder —
to acknowledge their power.

Shh, don't run. It's okay.
Wait. Breathe. Count to ten.
        See? They're gone.

Trust me, I know their secret.
I used to run from them, too, but then I learned . . .
their power is in the screech.
It's in the flapping. The dive-bombing.
The cloud of black they make on the periphery while
they swoop down, en masse.

They can't peck. They can't bite.
They don't know how.

Suicidality and addiction have a lot in common.

Your addiction is death.

And it has a heroin-sized grip on you.

Last Call

"Are you afraid? However could you not be?"
— Mumford & Sons, "Beloved"

It's dark and starless out.

I get up from bed when you call and go downstairs to the living room where a fire is smouldering, and the lights are dim enough that they don't bother this ever-present headache.

"Hey, doll."

"Hey. How's it going?"

You sound like yourself. Like you used to, years ago.

It's been three years since I've seen your face or touched you. Three years since you hugged me so tight and said, "Love of my life," and I walked down the stairs of our clinic apartment and out the door because I didn't want to see you pack your things into the car. Three years since I've looked into your eyes or put my hands through your hair.

And hearing your voice tonight, it seems like time has stood still. I remember so clearly who you used to be. Natalie says she's gone, the old you, but I don't think so. You're still there, somewhere, bound and gagged.

"God, this is such a fucking disaster, isn't it?"

"Little bit, yeah." And you laugh softly.

"What?"

And you say, "I've always wondered how such a sweet girl could have such a trucker's mouth."

And I laugh, because it's true, but so do you.

"Hey. We're going to figure this out. There is a solution. It's going to be okay."

And if I could rewind. . .

If I could stop time and
come back here, I would have

laid down my weapons

alongside yours and
crouched down beside you to
see the monster
pinning you flat
to the ground,
and I would have known
that

it

was

too

late

and that you had
                    already lost

and that in this one,
last moment,
all you needed was someone to
bear witness to the end.

To wave you free.

Do you want to stop the treatment?
Do you want to come home for this last part?
Are you afraid?

At least we could have said goodbye.

But I say, "Just keep breathing."
And you say, "I will. I love you."
And we hang up.

And I don't see you take your lifeline off your wrist and tie it around your neck.

That night, I dream of you, all dressed up like Before. You hold out two hands and I clasp them. You're nervous, you say, but excited. You're starting something new. Your face is glowing and healthy and you're smiling.

Day Thirty-Two

February 5

9:15

I know bilateral is hard but you can
do this. And if it's brutal, just remember,
you're one step closer to being finished.

1:12

Hey — are you up yet?

2:18

Are you alive, my dear?

4:53

"Yes, but I wish I wasn't?"
"Fuck off and don't talk to me?"
"I ran away, don't tell anyone?"
Choose your own.

6:51

Where are you? Call me.

8:05

I hope you're okay, doll.
It's not like you to go dark all day.
I'm here if you need me.

9:07

Goodnight . . . ?

🌙

On Friday morning, you went for your treatment,

    called your not-quite-husband,

        took a shoelace,

            locked the door to the shower room,

                and hung yourself.

Jesus fuck.

Shh. Don't talk to me. I can't breathe.

No.

I sit in the stupid shallow bathtub and sob. I leave the house with wet hair in February and walk around the block, stumbling in the wind coming off the ocean.

What the fuck have you done?

Steph?

Don't talk to me. She can't be dead.

She's not dead. She's still . . . the scan says . . . it might be . . .

What?

Catastrophic but not fatal.

No.

She might . . . she might just have brain damage. Maybe severe.

That's worse.

     THAT'S WORSE.

Jesus Christ.

Train tracks, Mack trucks, pills, and the hangman's noose.
Clearly you want to die.
But clearly some other force doesn't want you to because
you're still not fucking dead, are you?

You're still a little bit alive.

How much alive is the question.

And the answer is . . . we don't know.

They're going to pull the plug and we're going to wait.

Please don't leave me. I can't imagine a world without you in it.

He said he'd want them to pull the plug.

They didn't listen.

Fuck.

God. If you exist . . . please just let her die already.

I play your text tone over and over and over again. Because I know this is the last time I'll hear it while you're still on this earth.

*"But I was late for this, late for that,
late for the love of my life.
And when I die alone, when I
die alone, when I die I'll be on time."*
— The Lumineers, "Cleopatra"

Your dad drives down.
He signs the papers.
They take your organs.
They turn the machine off.

Peacefully, in hospital, with her partner and father by her side.

Right.

I hate being this far away from
you. Missing you is one of the
saddest parts of my life.

 I miss you terribly, too.

I know there are a lot of
things we don't talk about and
have never worked out, but I
have never stopped caring about
you for a second. If I could be
there, I would.

I know, and you are.

But I wasn't.

And now you're not, either.

I call Natalie and we sit on the phone and sob.

"Sometimes I wonder if I ever really knew her."

"I think you were the only one who really did."

Superheroes Don't Die Like This

This can't be the ending.

I keep waking up, thinking there must be a way to make this unhappen. To pick a different page on this choose-your-own-adventure. That somehow, this isn't the last page — it's just a warning of what could happen if we don't find the right storyline.

A.   They never take you off the Pill.

B.   I never leave for Curaçao.

C.   I confront your friends. The ones who are holding court behind your back, whispering and wondering *what the fuck* . . . [Yeah, I did that. Full Gladiator style. It didn't work. But I didn't know then how much hate and fear and jealousy are all entwined and that maybe I should have just said, *I'm afraid for her too* . . .]

D.   I tell your stepmother not to give up your practice. Not to let you sell the place. [You wanted to. You just don't remember. You were too sick to see people and you couldn't leave them without a doctor. You gave it up for them.]

E.   I never write you that letter. We never "break up." [But then you wouldn't have taken me seriously, would you? You would have kept me like your teddy bear, like the Giving Tree. Like a confessional you could carry around and drop whenever you liked . . .]

F.   I come to kidnap you in the middle of the night and bring you home. [But you never told me. You didn't say a word until it was too late and I'd moved halfway across the country and then you said it. *I hate my fucking life*. And I couldn't come to get you. I couldn't do anything but listen to you fall apart. Maybe that's why you finally said it.]

G.   I come keep you company on the psych ward.

That's impractical.

I come anyway. [Why is everything impractical? If it would keep someone fucking alive then it should have been considered, right? Or are we just interested in *practical* measures for saving lives? You know — the ones that don't fucking work?]

H).   I bring you out here, to our farmhouse by the ocean, to our barn
      full of animals, to our new life. I don't know the hows, but I do it
      anyway. And you walk down the beach with the sun on your face,
      and at night you put your head on my shoulder and I hold you
      tight and you finally breathe out. [COVID. **COVID**. THE WORLD WAS
      CLOSED FOR COVID.]

Fuck it. Let's do it then. We go all the way back to the first meeting.

"Take me back to the day we met."

And never meet.

You could have not made me laugh and I could have not made you cry, and
we could never have held hands or saved each other.

We could have never created this lifeline we needed to pull you out of those
deep pits you kept finding.

You could be happy right now in your undisturbed life. I could be happy right
now, too.

But my soul would still ache for you, I think.

And your life would still suffocate you.

We could have missed it all.

                                        But then we would have missed it all.

And what the fuck is life for if not to put your whole heart into something
that costs you your sanity and your sleep and your time and your safety, only
to end up broken and exhausted but *alive* because you had something worth
going to the ends of everything

to lose?

Breaths stand in for conversation.

Each exhale sounds like a directive to return.
But I can't see past the walls I keep hitting.

The phone chimes,
        but it's not you,
        so I ignore it because . . .
        because.

Natalie is texting that she wants me to get up and go outside

but she can't make me because of COVID and distance and the fact that last time we talked she pushed me too hard, and I got angry with her which has never happened before, but then again, you've never died before, so I guess there is no precedent.

Do you think we should make her get up?
Leave her. She'll get up when she's ready.

                       And whatever lens we've viewed this
                       marriage through,
                       whatever we've pretended
                       to see,
                       the glass is
                       spidering now,
                       because my love for you is
                       magnified tenfold
                       by your absence . . .

Breath in.

        Breath out.

How many in a day?

Do you want eggs?
Do you want tea?

                     No.

                     No.

I'm going now.

Okay.

Hey, P.S.: How much time off did you take?

Not enough.

Did you . . . tell them?

I had to. What else was I going to say?

Elegy for a Warrior Queen

"I had all and then most of you,
some and now none of you.
Take me back to the night we met."
– Lord Huron, "The Night We Met"

The sun is rising earlier and setting later. The ocean roars in the background of my life and I have stood by its edge and thrown rocks into its swells and screamed at it and cried. I have walked the beach every day, trying to parse this life you had — this final, devastating, irrevocable decision.

I've thought of walking into the water with rocks in my pockets and slipping under the surface of the ice floes because

what the hell is the point

if life is just this monster that grows hungrier by the year, demanding ever more of the people and things you love?

I have stood at the window and stared at the rope that hangs from the tree. In the summer, we attach a swing to it, but now it hangs like an empty noose, and I can't look away — even toward the ocean.

Where are you?

Your friends have sent me messages, shocked and stunned, wanting to know what the hell happened. What went so terribly wrong? How could they not have known something — especially this — was the matter with you? They're heartbroken and betrayed.

Your dark side was all I saw for years, so I don't know how to answer them except to say: *She didn't want people to know.* All while thinking, *How could anyone not see it?* That demon on your shoulder was so huge and heavy. The you we knew and loved was gone for so long . . . didn't they realise a doppelgänger was standing in your place?

The pit calls me, and I return to it day after day. Maybe my mind is still searching for you and that's the last place you were. All I want to do is curl up in the spot you lived in and sink. But I can't be down there alone. It's too dark. I fight to get out, even when it's pulling me back by the ankles.

It never leaves my mind, the image of you closing that bathroom door and locking it. Your hand-fashioned noose. Desperation. I'm haunted by your despair. Your loneliness. Your determination to die. I'm devastated by the loss of you. Not just now, but over all the years to come. I'm thirty-seven years old. If I live to be an old woman, how many decades is that without you? How many anniversaries and birthdays and holidays?

The thought makes me sick. Your absence chokes me.

If all you can do for the next two weeks is pop Ativan and do breathing exercises, it will be one of the most heroic acts of your life.

It will.

So I breathe.

And I wait for the ice pick in my stomach to dislodge. And the faucet in my heart to stop flooding my body with tears. My therapist says not to drink so much but I drink wine by the glass and rum by the snifter and wait to go to sleep.

My daughter kisses my cheek and I cup her face and tell her she's amazing and irreplaceable and she smiles and leaves me to cry.

And the hours pass.
    And the days pass.
        And it's a month since you died, except I really don't know what to count as your death:

                              the day you decided to die

                              or the day they decided to let you.

In the mornings, I get up early now. I greet the sun. I make tea silently and sit and stare out the window, a zombie drunk on sunlight . . . but at least I'm up.

At least I'm alive.

At least I didn't follow you into the dark.

That's all I can promise for now. When the sun is high and I know it will be least frigid, I pull on my boots and hat and trudge up the laneway to the beach road. I throw more rocks and trip up the stone shore, sit down on the boulders around the lighthouse, and sob.

I look at my phone, expecting it to chime.

I understand the phrase "every fibre of my being." My fibres carry your loss: my bones and my blood and my soul.

They carry your final confessions: the secrets you gave me and the ones you could only trust that I knew without saying. The things you couldn't release and took with you to your grave.

Your final directives speak volumes to me but nobody else is listening.

Spread my ashes behind my old house. Take me down to the ridge. Let me come home.

And I think: if I died, I wouldn't want them to bring me home. I'd want them to toss my ashes here on the waves where I feel you the most.

In the quiet of the evening, with the fire on and the freezing rain hitting the windowpane, I think of you running the trails behind your homestead, breathing in the deep woods and the smell of the turning leaves. I hear you whispering the Lord's Prayer under your breath, taking your demon in a chokehold.

You're my lifeline right now.
I know. I'm here.

Life is flat.

Grey.

And soundless.

But it keeps going.

It's insulting, really.

Dad texts to say he wants to talk to me.
He has news. He needs it to be kept
between us. It's medical. It's bad.

And in my head, I scream, *No. Do not
tell me.*

I don't want to know.

*I am not your secret keeper — the guardian
of the crypt.*

Please, tell someone else.

I was an orphan for seventeen years
and I managed that. I managed *all that*
without you.

Please don't come back for this.

I don't want anyone else's final days.

My sister calls him instead and says,
gently,

This probably isn't a good time . . .

The school calls and wants me to . . .
What?
Volunteer for what?

Hot chocolate day?
No. I . . .
I can't see people.

But if I don't go, it will be cancelled and hasn't everything already been cancelled enough?

COVID cancels everything, whether or not it's logical.

Whether it's a matter of "safety" or of optics or of people preferring to stay home all day because how are they supposed to come in to work when their own kids are home from school, so maybe it's just easier to cancel art classes even though they could easily be done six feet apart with masks and might have saved your life because #hope and #routine were two of the fundamental building blocks to your #sanity, no matter how precarious.

What if this hot chocolate day is some kid's art class?

Yes. Okay.
Fine, I'll do it.
Yes, I'm sure.
Yes, I'm sure you did hear.

Wednesday.
Wednesday.
Okay, Wednesday.

Hi.

        Hi.

I'm surprised to see you here, but thankful. It means so much to the . . .

                Right. Thanks. Sorry, just want to say, yes, I got your message, but I haven't been . . . just eating and breathing this week. Basics.

I'm in awe of that. Really.

                Thanks.

She's looking at me again.
Why?

I back away.

      I'm sorry, did I
accidentally leave the door
open?

It's supposed to be
locked shut.

My person has died.
      I don't need visitors to this
train wreck.

Disaster tourism is rude.

But she just smiles.

I'm so sorry.
My heart and my thoughts and my prayers
have been with you.

And I think — who the hell are you?

Even though she's been in my periphery: a side character to this story for the past half year,
in and out of the plot like a hummingbird feeding and retreating.

I just haven't had time to notice.

I don't even know you.

But some whisper reflects back from
that corner of the universe that
knows all things . . .

Not yet.

Can I catalogue your faults instead?
The things that make me angry, years later?

      Because it's been years and I'm still angry,
      which is better. And worse.
            Worse, mostly. But sometimes a relief

      because I don't miss your
carelessness or your thoughtless words or your
lies.

I don't miss the way you used people,
      the fact that you forgot my birthday
or never learned it.

         The way you shut up and shut down and shut off
instead of just doing hard things.

The way you told me you needed saving
when there was no way I could save you

And then didn't say goodbye.

If I think of those things, I can still
think of you

Without this bottomless ache.

I watch *Grey's* alone. I never liked it as much as you did but it's COVID. It's still COVID. COVID is going on and on and fucking on even though the vaccines are here, and the antivirals are being developed. We're all still in the Netflix & Chill cycle so . . .

Couch.

Grey's.

And I think, if you were alive, you could have seen Meredith wake up, but you're dead so you can't. So fuck you — I'll drink my margarita and yours, and I won't miss you. You're not visiting me in my dreams or in signs from the universe.

Maybe because you know I don't want to see you.

> Because I can barely breathe as it is without having you popping in to say hello

> > then vanishing again.

Except that you're talking to me now in McDreamy's voice.

> > (Next, I'll put on my tin foil hat and glue newspaper over my windows.)

But really . . . you are.

"I never understood the level of exhaustion. There comes a point where the desire to rest overrides the desire to live."

Just like that, your choice was made.
Just like that, the branch broke.
Just like that, you're gone.

No resolution. No happy ending. No ending at all except you out the airlock, free-floating in space . . .

Escape hatch activated.

Bail out.

I walk along the beach.

. . . the desire to rest overrides the desire to live . . .

Collect handfuls of mini jellyfish,
perfect oval sacs
glistening like melted ice
along the red sand,

Toss them up and over
the waves,

Watch the gulls dive.

Counsellor: Do you want to talk about it?

Me: What for?

Counsellor: Don't you think talking helps?

Me: No. I don't. All we did was talk. Talk and talk and talk all fucking day until she could finally turn the lights off at night. Because the waking hours were such a struggle that bailing out was the only relief. You say to name things to manage them but calling this monster by its name didn't kill it. Talking about her struggles didn't end them, did it? It just prolonged her life.

Counsellor: Is there any value in that?

Me: What? More time?

Counsellor: The last month. The fact that she didn't succeed in January.

Me: The fact that she had to suffer through a month of ECT and then died anyway . . . ?

Counsellor: Do you think she would have wanted to give you that time? That closure? Even if she was suffering?

Me: I don't know. I don't feel "closed" about it. I feel unmoored and unsafe and if I'd known that it would end like this, don't you think I would rather she'd just gone to sleep with the pills?

Counsellor: Would you? How would you have dealt with the guilt if she'd died then?

Me:

Counsellor: She could have gone home. She knew that. But she chose to stay. Why?

Me: Because she knew that at home it would be too easy. She was giving herself a fighting chance by staying in the hospital.

Counsellor: Okay. So she fought and she lost. Sometimes people lose.

Me: Yeah. Just like a baseball game.

Counsellor: You know that's not what I meant.

Me: I lost, too.

Counsellor: "You can't save people. You can only love them."

Me: That's just what you tell people so they can sleep at night.

Counsellor: If people can be saved, it's not one conversation or one moment of clarity that's going to do it. It's many conversations over many hours over many days.

Me: My point. That's what we had.

Counsellor: And maybe, no matter what, Steph — all roads led here. But what I do think is that your willingness to go into the pit with her was what allowed her to hang on for so long.

Me: It looks nothing like people think down there. Nothing.

Counsellor: If you could tell people what it looks like . . . what would you say? What would you want them to know?

Me: Honestly? Who cares? Knowing doesn't stop anything, does it? Everyone around her fucking knew she wanted to die. She killed herself *at a psychiatric hospital*. How does knowing help? How does raising awareness help? We were aware.

She. Is. Still. Dead.

Counsellor: Okay, but you're not.

Me: Let's not, okay?

Drowning Doesn't Look Like Drowning

Me: Okay. Fine. This is what I would want people to know.

Drowning doesn't look like drowning.
      There are no dramatic cries, arms flailing, or
bodies surging out of the surf.

Drowning is silent — a slipping under the surface, surrounded
by people laughing
and throwing beach balls.

Drowning doesn't sound like drowning.
It sounds like *I'm fine* and *I'm sorry, I can't make it tonight.*
        Tomorrow?

It sounds like a thousand deep and shaky breaths
before a
          sob.
It sounds like crying in the shower.

Drowning doesn't feel like
      drowning. It feels
like life just put on some
weight and
suddenly you're sinking.

It feels like ninety glaring sunrises
after three months of sleepless
      nights and hours of
therapy and hundreds of
         cups of tea gone cold
on the nightstand while you

Stare at the wall
    and think . . .

I know drowning doesn't look like drowning,
and I was your
lifeline to the shore, so
why did you tell me to throw the rope
and then not catch it?

Goodbye doesn't sound like
goodbye.
It doesn't sound like us.
It doesn't sound like forever.

It sounds like
I'll talk to you later.
Hang in there.
Stay strong, doll.

It sounds like
Hey, it's me.

Then there was the day you sent that great shaggy dog to goose me on the main road.

I have no words.

I am still laughing.

I felt you that day. The only time I did. The only time you said hello.

Well . . . for a while.

Before you started sending shooting stars.

First, the angel.

Then the sister.

Then the lover.

No, I Don't Want a Friend

What? Again?

There she is, wings tapping lightly on my door.

Gentle smile and warm eyes — so bright and alive above the mask.

I frown.

Hi. What's up?

She winks.

> *You bring so much joy and laughter to my life.*

And I just stare because I can't remember a single joyful, funny word I've said to her
or any words at all except
hello, and *thank you*, and *can I get you a cup of coffee*
because I'm not a professor just now but a barista in a fishing village and everyone knows everyone six different ways,

And she's crossed my path but I've never really noticed

how sad she is.

                                        Hello?

Hello.

Is there something you need?

                                        Maybe.
                                        A friend?
Someday.
But it can't be you.

                                        Why not?

Because.
I can't even tell you who I am right now so,
Nice to meet you in this
identity twilight zone,
this grey space somewhere between
not anymore and
not yet. Where she's dead
and so much of me has gone with her except
                                I still want my life —
at least I think I do. Even if I'm not fighting very hard for it.

A dying phoenix,
          not yet risen.
                    Probably defective.
                              Welcome to my pile of ashes.

But listen, if you do need to talk to someone . . .
It's just that I've noticed that . . .
It's none of my business, but it seems like you might not have anyone else
so . . .

Just hold, please, while I close this last
chapter because the last person I
talked to never finished the conversation
but it's just a flaw in me that I have to
hear you out . . .

                                        Okay

And that's when I look closer.
That's when I see it.

The hole she's treading water in.
Fathoms deep and silent.

And I reach out
because it's a reflex, even if it's a fatal one.

Can I help?

And she whispers,

Please don't tell anyone but
I think I'm drowning.

Right.
I know the feeling.

I shouldn't be here.
On the other end of someone's lifeline.
It's too much and too soon and too wrong.

But she's so light in comparison to you.

She swims.

And she says,
Your friendship is an answer
     to prayer.

And I stare at her words,
an answer
     to prayer,

Wondering what she's been

praying for.

I didn't want another person.
If I'd known she wasn't going to knock first,

I would have put the deadbolt on.

And she sips her tea and crosses her legs.
Shrugs and smiles.
She's wrapped in a muslin robe,
celestial hair still wet from the plunge.

I don't know what made me . . .
I don't usually . . .
never actually

What? Talk?

To anyone.

I'm so grateful for you.
You don't even know.
You're such a light.

Maybe that's why I'm so

blindsided.

No. Nobody Else.

But the next one knocks on my door, and I sit down.
In the store or
on the phone, late at night,
years of grief tumbling out
in jumbles of tears and words,
and I lean against the pillows and listen,
breathe,
say, "Breathe, it's okay,"
and wait.

Because I know how to hold space. I have been holding space with you for
years. Waiting for you to come back to yourself and fill it up.

It's an aching muscle, my listening ear.
But I ask questions, gently
plucking confessions like ripe
pomegranate seeds from their
papery husks,
remembering how yours were more like
excisions of teeth
leaving raw, open craters . . .

And after a quick untying —
a sharp yank to release
each knot —
it's done. Unburdened.
Nothing at all like the weight
of the web you carried,
sopping wet and impossibly tangled.

At night, when I try to sleep, my brain turns it all over, pulling the pieces
up one by one, working to unknot them, up and over and around the whole
matted mess.

Wondering how on earth it got that way . . .

how we couldn't free you.

And, listening instead of speaking, I make the days pass.

One hundred and twelve sunsets.

Sixteen weeks of *Grey's Anatomy.*

One Cinco de Mayo.

And another text message on my screen from her.

Not the angel or the sister.

Nope.

This one doesn't fit a box.

·   She never did.

I miss home. The lakes and the forests. The loon calls at sunrise before the bell rang and all the campers lined up at the flagpole for *Salutation to the Dawn*.

This ocean is someone else's childhood. The heaving rocks and shoreline stacked with seaweed is the stuff their summers were made of. I don't belong here.

I need to be around people who don't gasp when I say *Jesus fucking Christ*.

Jesus fucking Christ.

I almost cried with relief when she said it,

to see her name again on my screen after an absence I hadn't noticed

                                        extending

until it was too late.

A dropping of the ball.

A slipping away of ties.

What the fuck happened?

                                        She died.

I don't think before I answer. Honesty with her has always been as knee-jerk
as the smile she pulls from me.

Like the day, years ago, when I told her about you. . .

Because? Because. . .

She asked me something,
which led to another thing,
which led to you,
and she sort of paused and gave me a
look.

I didn't know that look yet.

Her eyes are the colour of dark tequila while yours are mid-summer blue, and they smoulder when she's been drinking. Something you have in common.

But that comes later.

The night you died and your obituary came up all over social media, she was the first person to call, and her f-bombs gave me space to

take my first deep breath since

you stopped.

How *did she die?*
I'm so fucking sorry,
Steph.

Yeah. Same.

There are turning points to grief.

Doors you slip through and which, mercifully, close behind you.

When I hand the keys to her, each an entry to the endless portals of what-ifs,

she holds them for a moment,

turns them over,

says, *I think we can throw this one away now.*

And we close that door.

But I can't stop wandering the halls of our house of mirrors.

And I don't feel myself slipping

                                        sideways

through the false walls

until I'm lost.

Hey!

. . .

HEY!

                                        Hi. What?

PICK UP THE PHONE.

An insistent voice. Not gentle,
hesitant.
No.

She pins me to the wall with her words and makes me . . .

Stop. You need to stop.
Stop counting the days.
She's gone.

And from somewhere in the endless refracted

hallways, I follow her voice

out.

> *How? How do I stop?*
> *My body counts the heartbeats.*
> *I don't know how to not . . .*

Talk to her instead.
On the other side.

> *I don't know what that means.*
> *I don't know what's on the*
> *other side.*

Just pretend she's across a veil
somewhere. Picture her as an
archangel. Whatever.
Just stop. Please.

Breathe.
In. Out. In.

> *Okay.*

And then setting day comes and the
boats go out
and the catch starts coming in.
The wharf is alive with noise and the community
erupts in.

Summer.

Lobster rolls and oysters on the half shell,
tourists allowed, double-vaxxed,
past the drawbridge.

And the sun rises early, setting late
over bonfires,
waves at high tide
crashing up to douse the
final embers.

I stop trying to untangle the web.
I stop trying to make it unhappen.

I hold your hand on the beach and talk to you instead, out loud, wondering if
anyone is listening, thinking I'm crazy for talking to a ghost . . . and if you can
really hear me.

We sit on the piece of driftwood at the point and I tell you . . .

I tell you,

finally,

I am so sorry.
And I love you.
And I'm sorry for loving you some days.

And my body still counts the breaths you're not taking.

I can stop counting but

my soul is still missing. It's attached to you.

And I ask again . . .

What good is a body in a marriage

Without a soul?

And so I finally let the marriage go, too.

Rocks skipped over the glassy surface.

Shells thrown into the chop.

How much more can I let go?

All of it?

I might like to let go of

all of it.

I might like to let go of you.

Can you go first?

Oh wait.

I don't know where to go next;

I don't know what to do now that all the balls

in the air
are
on the floor.

Wife

Mother

Friend

Almost-lover

You said, when your dying was a theory, not my daily news bulletin . . .

You'll miss me, but then you'll get over it. You'll move on. You'll live your life without the burden of . . .

I can't remember the rest.

Except to say — those three words? *You'll move on?*

I feel you missed some steps there.

Fuck you. I'm not playing this game.

I'm done picking up the pieces in life.
I am not starting over.

No.

I just want to stop thinking.

It's summer and the nights are long and I'm cycling out of losing you and cycling into losing everything else and—

What the fuck?

Are you serious right now?

I said I was done.

But you're doing that thing I used to do

to you and . . .

Sorry. Override.

I'm sending you someone you don't even know you need.

In the hollow spaces you've left, she reaches out for me.

No.

I don't want to talk.

That's okay. I'll talk now.

I miss talking to you.

I miss you.

And now we're talking and texting like we used to,

before I moved away to her home province, and she felt left behind and not-brave-enough.

Her parents are aging, and she feels too far away because #COVID and #Restrictions. Her voice is raspier than I remember — teaching in a mask for a year — but hearing it on the other end of the line is new and familiar and safe and warm and . . . and . . .

Why did we stop talking?

> *Because you stopped answering. You were mad.*

I was?

> *I thought you were.*

I don't remember.
I'm sorry.
I want to be there for you.

And now she texts me like she used to. Except it's different.

Now I'm braver because I know what it's like to lose someone without ever having said . . .

> `I can't live without you.`

We need rules.

                              Yeah? Like — we should
                                probably never be
                             alone in a hotel room
                                    together? ;)

Maybe . . . :)

And then suddenly she stops texting and calling and

just gets in the truck,

dragging her sixteen-foot trailer all the way from home —

seventeen hours across rainy highways.

What do you mean you're coming to visit?

I mean I'm coming.

Really? Why?

*Because. Because
I have to see you.*

*I thought we agreed:
no hotel rooms.*

*I'll sleep
outside.*

. . . and in the next breath, she arrives on my doorstep. Like a present you've
giftwrapped.

Same ripped stomach,
same ripped jeans.

I stare at her Ray-Bans, shoved into her dark curls,
blue tint reflecting blue sky,

feel my breath catch in the way she looks at me
and, more than that,

the way you've
pulled the stars together

then sent one hurtling past the moon at
just the moment I woke up and looked
outside.

A familiar face,

with an unfamiliar worry line in the centre of her forehead.

Hey.

Hey.

Can you . . .

can you actually bend
time and place
because

five years of friendship just turns on a dime, and now we're walking the
beach, hand in hand, like we've always belonged together and

she's picking up the pieces I've dropped

along the way,

Stopping at the edge of the water to
look at me and . . .

Fuck.

Really?

Why? Why did you come?

                                        Because I was worried.
                            Because I thought . . . you might . . .

What?

                                I thought you might give up, too.
                                                Without her.

                                And I couldn't stand that.

But when she leans in to kiss me, I put my hand on her chest.

No.

Please don't.

You have to promise not to do that.

So for the next few days, we just walk the red sand and talk.

And I wonder what the fuck you were thinking with this particular present.

Funny that you'd send me someone who hated you.

You broke her ankle in a soccer game once, but you didn't remember
that one time I asked you.

Before. When we were friends, and not

This.

She remembers, though. Jesus.

Rec soccer outdoors with all those athletic women thundering up and down a
field in pursuit of a black and white checked ball to hammer home . . . except
it was a field of ligaments you hammered home.

> *Your dead girlfriend?*
> *She was an asshole.*

She smiles when she says it and puts a hand on my face. Her eyes search me
for signs I'm going to break.

But I don't.

I need to stop breaking.

You were an asshole.
But fuck, I loved you.

Her hands are warm on my back.

And when I
turn out the light and
step into the space
that holds us,

she waits, still, for me
to break the promise I

made her keep.

Is it weird?

What?

She traces a line down my spine in the dark and cups her hand around my neck while we're falling asleep. Her voice is almost normal at a whisper. Almost the way I remember, from Before.

That I think she was the reason . . .

                                                                    What?

That all this happened? That I came for you?

I don't answer right away because . . . because.

My body hasn't stopped feeling the water creeping up.
How easy it is to slip under.

Drowning doesn't look like drowning. . .

But she knew.

                                        No. It's not weird.
                        You were the only one who could've . . .

What?

                                                Gotten through.

August

September

October

November

December

January

February

March

April

May

And now every night as we're lying on the couch, I have to rotate that ankle in my hands, stopping just before she winces, and rotating it back the other way. All so that she can keep moving . . . because her head is like your head and only settles into submission when it's exhausted from exercise.

And I look at her sometimes because I know what happens to athletic girls who stop running.

But when I'm done, she looks at me with those smoky tequila eyes and says, "Thanks."

And

"I love you."

Shine On

"I crossed all the lines and I broke all the rules,
But baby, I broke them all for you."
— Brandi Carlile, "The Story"

It's your smile that I will take with me for the rest of this journey.
The rest can go.

When I'm old and sitting in a rocking chair, facing the ocean, with drones
overhead dropping groceries in mushroom fibre boxes to people along the
shore in the moments before the flying car comes to pick me up for my
memory-care appointment, I will remember that megawatt smile.

I have a box for the rest: the bracelet that we used to swap out every time
you went into hospital and recovered — the one I've worn since you died;
the necklace you brought me from Prague; the playing cards and the journal
from the second care package I never got to send; the picture of you on top
of that giant horse; the shirt we shared; the notes you left me; the letters I
wrote you; the painting I asked for to replace the one I burned.

One day, if that box doesn't move with me, wherever I'm going, that's okay.

I just want to remember that shine. The thing that rubbed off on everyone
you touched. The light that burned my skin. It's what I remember best from
Before. What I held in my mind during all your dark days, and what I will
remember when the details fade — because they will — and all I will get to
hold onto is something I can't close my hands around.

Hey.

Don't forget
the tequila.

When the other back wheel comes off my tricycle, trundling down the road,
off-balance and squeaking, and I lose it on the side of the road — first you to

suicide, then her to divorce — I breathe and walk and let go and release and feel you with me.

When the days stretch out in this endless black tunnel; when the rain is so heavy, and the hours are so long and dark, and my body aches with sadness, and my mind can't wrap around the idea of never picking up and hearing you say, "Hey," I put my hand into that pocket of sunshine you always kept on hand.

And I start giving it away.

Gifts and notes and compliments and memories and encouragement and pep talks and soup and cookies and books and candles and everything. Everything to put your light back out into the world.

And when people say thank you, I just smile at them like you would, and I say,

Shine on.

Because when I don't want to get out of bed some days, I remember how you always did — every single day until the last one.

When I can't sleep because I'm thinking of all the things I still want to say to you, and should have said, and still need to say, I remember you up a ladder, grinning down at me as you splashed paint from the roller. Behind the wheel of that monster truck. Whipping aside the curtain of a changeroom to show me your new perfect jeans. Taking a bite of my lemon soup and grimacing. Hugging me tight. Saying, *Goodnight, my dear friend. Sweet dreams.*

I let them have their moments and their farewells, their fantasies and their questions. I let them wear their rose-coloured glasses, blinded to all rainbows. Their reality was not mine and that's made me question everything about you & me for as long as we've been a you & me, but these are the things I know:

You were a beautiful soul. A complicated mind. A warrior and an angel.

You loved me to the depths of your soul. I loved you the same.

There are no do-overs. No reconciliations. We had the time we had and now it's over.

And now I have to live the rest of it all without you.

Steph,

Words cannot express enough the love and gratitude I feel towards you for saving my life (literally and figuratively). People come and go in our lives and some remain forever. You're one of my forevers.

Thank you from the bottom of my heart.

S